THE MA FAMILY CHINESE COOKBOOK

THE MA FAMILY
CHINESE COOKBOOK

Nancy Chih Ma
Irene Tsoi Ma
Mary Ma Stavonhagen
Helen Ma Yamawaki

Photographs by Yoshiya Fukuda

KODANSHA INTERNATIONAL LTD.
Tokyo, New York & San Francisco

Previously published as *Don't Lick the Chopsticks*

Distributors:

UNITED STATES: Harper & Row, Publishers, Inc., 10 East 53rd
Street, New York, New York 10022. CANADA: Fitzhenry &
Whiteside Ltd., 150 Lesmill Road, Don Mills, Ontario M3B 2T5.
MEXICO AND CENTRAL AMERICA: Harla S.A. de C.V., Apartado
30–456, Mexico 4, D.F. SOUTH AMERICA: Harper & Row,
Publishers, Inc., International Department. UNITED KINGDOM:
Phaidon Press Ltd., Unit B, Ridgeway Trading Estate, Iver,
Bucks SLO 9HW. EUROPE: Boxerbooks Inc., Limmatstrasse 111,
8031 Zurich. AUSTRALIA AND NEW ZEALAND: Book Wise (Aus-
tralia) Pty. Ltd., 104–8 Sussex Street, Sydney 2000. ASIA: Toppan
Company (S) Pte. Ltd., 38 Liu Fang Road, Jurong Town,
Singapore 2262.

Published by Kodansha International Ltd., 12-21, Otowa 2-
chome, Bunkyo-ku, Tokyo 112 and Kodansha International/
USA, Ltd., 10 East 53rd Street, New York, New York 10022
and 44 Montgomery Street, San Francisco, California 94104.
Copyright © 1973 by Kodansha International Ltd. All rights
reserved. Printed in Japan.

LCC 80–82528
ISBN 0–87011–435–2
JBC 2077–789129–2361

First printing, 1980

Contents

A Family is for Cooking

Nancy Chih Ma

風, 花, 雪, 月. "Wind," "flower," "snow," "moon." I love these words. In Chinese they look so romantic. God created the world; it is really beautiful. I wanted to be a writer to describe all the beauty and good and give what I owe to the great world. This was my desire when I was young. But it did not happen. I became a food writer.

I was born and grew up in Harbin, North China. Harbin was the gateway of Western culture through the Siberian Railway and was known as the little Paris of the Far East. Harbin was an international metropolis populated by English, American, French, Danish, Swedish, Dutch, White Russian, and other nationalities. I had the opportunity to receive culture from both East and West. This cosmopolitan population also influenced the food. My family's cook not only could cook Chinese food but also Russian food. Our lunch was always Russian, and dinner was Chinese.

It is not surprising mealtime was very special in China. Hardly a day passed when we did not have at least one guest for lunch or dinner. My mother never refused a visitor to join us. Housewives are likely to say that all she had to do was to add a pair of chopsticks to the table for each guest. My mother believed people get more than nutrition when eating good food. It is the time also for the family to share the day's experiences, adventures, happinesses, and sufferings. It is an aesthetic pleasure, a social occasion, a time for relaxation and conversation. I am thankful for all the feasts and daily meals when I was young. But I did not have the opportunity to enter the kitchens.

Besides the general subjects I learned in school, tutors also taught me English, Russian, music, and fifty small Chinese characters and twenty bigger ones a day. The experiences of daily life taught me that natural self-discipline and politeness must not be artificial. Warmth and sympathy must permeate; charm and gaiety must be extended to all. My parents also agreed with the maxim, "Study from traveling one thousand miles is better than study from one hundred books."

The phrase *hui niang chia* ("visiting mother's home") was one that brought joy to a girl's heart. This was the time when a married daughter made the trip back to her own home. My mother visited her parent's family twice a year, and of course I went along.

China's land is immense, yet crops never traveled far. The harvest of their own land showed in my grandparents' daily rice bowl. When the ground was frozen in winter, the farm horses and wagons were put to use hauling salt. I enjoyed watching them make their own soybean paste. Beans were boiled until soft, giving off a delicious odor as they boiled. Then five by five by three-inch bricks of boiled beans were made, allowed to ferment, soaked, and salt added. The fermented paste was placed in large earthenware jars, which were put on one side of the yard and covered with a hat of straw matting, double woven and decorated with a piece of red cotton material tied with red string. The sun's heat worked on the mixture, and after three days it was time for grandmother to open the hat and start to beat the paste. One hundred strokes were necessary every day for one month, then it was finished. Bean paste was the most important seasoning for the family. There were also a great variety of vegetables from the back garden, geese and ducks from the nearby pond, chickens and pigs from the farmyard, and pears and grapes from the orchard. Everything came from their own land. They worked hard to eat right. These are the most interesting memories of my childhood life.

My mother loved to make preserves and jams of strawberries and blueberries in season. She learned this from a Russian neighbor. She also put away all kinds of Chinese pickles in different porcelain jars and glass bottles, including salted duck and chicken eggs. It was one of her special loves to make preserved food for the family in preparation for winter. At that time, among the exotic dishes were braised shark's fins, bird's nest soup, Peking duck, suckling pig, steamed buns with chicken broth filling, and fish, one side of which was cooked, the other raw. I also remember braised chicken with wine, goose with apricots, turtle soup, and honey-ginger drink. The fresh cucumbers, eggplants, leeks, green peppers pickled lightly in homemade soybean paste were particularly nutritious. In old China, two hundred dishes could be served at a grand banquet. A proverb: three generations to know to dress well and four generations to understand good food. But I believe that from the time Adam first bit into an apple, good food must have developed quickly. We don't need four generations; we just need attention and love to cook the food. Wives who can cook well bring more happiness to the family. Cooks who cook well attract more friends.

Danny Kaye is a fascinating cook who only cooks for his friends. How he encouraged me! He cooked nine courses for us, this man whose minutes on television are worth thousands of dollars. "Cooking for friends is my pleasure," he said. Friendship is invaluable. His nice thoughts still warm my heart.

How I Create New Recipes
When Danny Kaye and I chatted about food, he mentioned how the kumquat is both cute and colorful. I thought about how Americans like spareribs. Using a heavy knife, I crushed the kumquats lightly to make the seeds pop out. Then I deep fried spareribs with kumquats and topped this with sweet and sour sauce. This dish not only looks beautiful, but tastes good.

When our friend Jiro Gadelius took us out to dinner in Stockholm, the famous snow grouse with meat sauce and shrimp gave me the idea to deep fry quail marinated in Chinese five spices. In Rome I found the idea to make my steamed Chinese cabbage layered with ground meat (Helen has a different recipe, included here, which she made up herself). The pastry of Copenhagen inspired my sweet dumplings filled with raisins and sesame seeds.

When I travel to various countries around the world, I never miss visiting the local markets. This is the best way to get in close contact with people and what they eat, and, besides, it is great fun. In 1964, when I first visited the U.S.A., the frozen rolls impressed me very much. I even took some back home to Tokyo (where frozen foods had not yet appeared on the domestic market) and continued to enjoy them until my supply ran out. In European markets, the displays of different kinds of cheeses attracted my eye. The effect was very different from the Chinese market, with its jars of dried things and prepared meats, roast duck, and smoked chicken hanging from steel hooks. Every kind of ingredient—whether fish, meat, vegetables, or fruit—their aromas, tastes, and colors require our love, our understanding, and our effort.

General Ben Davis's wife, Aggie, always adds one line to her Christmas card to me. "When will your new cookbook be out?" She has given me a great many Western cookbooks and has encouraged me to pick up the pen. But when I try to write a new recipe, I just like to sit imagining, dreaming, running the pen over the paper as if I were writing poetry, music, or painting—but recipes it is. Making food—washing, chopping, cutting, frying, steaming, seasoning—is the same as creating or enjoying the brilliance of music or painting.

I remember my childhood as a mixture of luxury and hard work. My parents wanted me to know the good things in life and how to enjoy them. But they also made sure that I studied hard and learned from the example of others and other countries. I was reminded always that I must work hard so that when I grew up I would not lose the good things I already had.

In Japan, when it came time to educate our children, I decided that I would not be satisfied with less than the best. One son, one daughter were educated in American schools; one son, one daughter in Japanese schools. After the two daughters graduated, I took them on a tour of America. Wherever we went, good friends took care of us; and they put my name in the local newspapers. When people found out that I was the author of Chinese cookbooks, they asked me to give cooking demonstrations on television. So my daughters had to assist me. They never had stage fright, helped me conscientiously, and received a great many compliments. This is how they received my cooking lessons—from the chance to teach cooking.

Then marriage time came. Mary's husband is German, and Helen's, Japanese. My husband was upset; of course everybody wants their children to choose a partner of their own culture and background. I knew it is a difficult problem. Because of their schools, all their friends were of various nationalities. Intermarriage was difficult to avoid. Though I hoped one or two children would marry Chinese, I tried to be very broad-minded. The love of lovers is indestructible. Now, five and seven years respectively have passed since the two weddings. Both girls and their husbands live satisfied, happy lives. It is a major thing. My husband is very proud of his two foreign sons-in-law.

Mary visits Europe to see her parents-in-law often. Her wide experience abroad has given her many ideas for food. Helen lives in Tokyo, where she has learned the secrets of Japanese cooking. Mary's son Thomas is three years old. Among his favorite foods are Chinese meat buns or sweet bean buns. This predilection must be inherited from his mother, since I often made these buns when my children were small. Of course he is a cheese eater also. Mary sometimes gets irritated and complains that the boy is too fussy about food. He knows what is good.

That my girls are interested in cooking is a pleasure to me. Good food helps make a happy family.

Our son Johnny was educated at the University of Arizona. When still in high school, he loved milk and European food. The first thing he did after coming home from school was open the refrigerator and have a cup of milk. When he left for America alone, I comforted myself that at least his beloved milk would not be lacking there.

He took a copy of my first cookbook with him. During his last year in university, one day I got a letter from him, which said, "I cooked a few dishes from your book. It works."

Time flies. After his graduation, Johnny worked in Los Angeles. In 1969, when we visited him there, he introduced us to a Chinese girl from Hong Kong. "Is she nice?" he asked me. Yes, she was charming, elegant, modern, and very warmhearted.

In 1970 we went to their wedding, which was held in beautiful Carmel, California. One of our Chinese friends shook my husband's hand and said, "Congratulations on your son's wedding. Your boy also married a foreigner." We Chinese are very conservative; even marriage to someone from a different part of China is considered difficult because of the differences in language and customs. Irene's family is from Swatow, where the people have their own dialect of Cantonese and where customs are different from other parts of Canton Province. Before she went to study at art school, Irene's mother taught her some cooking. Her mother is very domestic and a lovely lady. John is lucky to have married such a beautiful and capable girl. In China each province has its own way to cook; everyone welcomes new and unusual recipes from other areas. But Irene's art is not limited to cooking; she also is a talented designer and artist.

This book could have been written two years ago, but a mother should always extend her love to all her children equally. I have waited for the bride of the other son, Tom, to appear. But he is still a bachelor. Time, like the tide, rolls too quickly. Please allow us to present you with the cooking of this family and to express our joy while all the girls are not too far away.

A proverb: Yesterday is a memory, tomorrow is a dream, but today is a reality. Another proverb: When you don't know how to cook Chinese food, you stay put like a flower in a mirror or the moon in a stream, but when you understand the basics, you will travel a thousand leagues a day.

Swatownese Me

 Irene Tsoi Ma

I was born in Hong Kong, where the majority of the population is Cantonese speaking. Hong Kong is only 180 miles south of Swatow, but most elderly Swatownese in Hong Kong raise their families with Swatownese customs, Swatownese dialect is spoken at home, traditions observed, and the home cooking is Swatow. I was fortunate enough to belong to such a family. My earliest memory of being in close contact with the kitchen was when I was a little girl of around five or six. Somehow, I'd always been interested in cooking, perhaps because I liked to eat.

I can still see our cook laboring away in the dark kitchen on the gas stove, which she had been persuaded to use instead of the traditional charcoal stove. However, whenever any important guests were expected, the retired chef, who my grandfather had brought out with him from Swatow, was summoned to perform his magic. That was when the three or four small clay charcoal stoves were taken out of their hiding places and resumed their importance in the kitchen. I can visualize him now, that old magician, coming back from marketing in the morning with bulks of red meat, fresh vegetables, live fish, a live duck, and a live chicken, the last two quacking and clucking at the ends of bits of straw string. It was fascinating to a child. Nothing was killed until the very last moment, in order to provide the ultimate in freshness; the steamed fish on the platter had been flapping around forty-five minutes earlier.

Swatownese cooking is one of the many styles of Cantonese (Kwangtung) cuisine. Its characteristics are delicacy and freshness, which are utilized to appeal not only to the palate but also to sight and smell. With modern refrigeration (for short periods), good Swatownese food can now be made by anyone. When the fundamentals are mastered, Swatownese cuisine is as simple as any. And with a little imagination, you will find yourself inventing your own Swatownese dishes. I have chosen some very simple and some more complicated dishes, besides a few Hong Kong Cantonese dishes, in order that you may taste and enjoy.

Swatow food is one of the gourmet cuisines of China, and, in Hong Kong, to dine Swatownese is to expect a meal of excellence and elegance. It is also among the most expensive restaurant cuisines because of its quality and freshness. I hope that with the publication of this book, people will come to understand that Cantonese cooking constitutes numerous types and will give it the credit it deserves, since lately this cuisine has been obscured by the other regional styles. To give my aunt a plug, a very good cross section and variety of Cantonese food is presented in *Chinese Home Cooking*, by Nancy Chih Ma's sister Julia Cheng. Gone are the days when Cantonese cooking conjures up almond chicken and sweet and sour pork solely.

As a teenager, I knew a little Swatownese cooking, together with some Cantonese, due to my mother's skill. But the crash course came when I was to leave for studies in the United States, where I knew the only Swatownese home cooking I could taste would be my own. I liked American food, for I had lived there before. In fact, my family had traveled through Europe and had spent some time in South America. I enjoyed most of the food in every country I visited. But there is no food like mother's.

For three months before I left, first I helped her, then, finally, I cooked a whole five-course dinner. It was a time of fun and laughter, of dismay over accidents and failures, then of joy and pride of success. Confidence and enthusiasm grew when my skills were appreciated and complimented. Then courses would resume every time I came home for the holidays. However, the climax of my learning came when I got married and returned to live in Hong Kong.

When I married John, Nancy and Paul Ma's youngest son and the darling of a family of cooks, he had a strong conviction that Pekinese food was the most truly authentic and most delicious of all Chinese cooking. But, after introducing him to Swatownese food, he now responds with the same satisfied smile that his familiar northern cooking evokes, even if he won't admit that Swatownese cooking is superior. Imagine my delight, then, when Nancy Ma, my famous and lovely mother-in-law, invited and encouraged me to write a section of this book.

Und Mit Sauerkraut

 Mary Ma Stavonhagen

Among my earliest memories are the nostalgic recollections of life in a large Chinese family, with the grandparents dominating one and all. Yet, small as I was, I seemed already to realize how much life did center around us, the youngest generation. Especially with my brothers. Grandfather would come home hollering and singling out "his eldest grandson or his number two grandson." That doesn't imply that the female members were without authority. On the contrary, I, as the eldest, during our teenage years was expected to represent our generation at social functions. There, my education outside the schoolroom broadened. I was, for the first time, on my own to meet and mingle with grownups, to listen, speak, and learn from them. Now, I realize it must be there that I learned to socialize, to be able to carry on an interesting conversation, how to dress appropriately for each occasion, etc. This was the gentle push that I needed to enable me to leave my family much later to further my studies in far-away Switzerland.

Our mealtimes were always noisy affairs carried around a round table, which seated anywhere from ten to fifteen people. Each of us had his permanent seat. I, being the eldest, sat between father and grandmother. And always each child sat between two adults in order to keep down our chatter and nonsense. The meal itself was always plentiful and varied. The seasons seemed to be dictated by the dishes served. When we had the "Ma family sandwiches," braised bamboo with pork, etc., it was sure to be spring. Summers, instead of tea, plum tea was served to take away the heat from the body, and steamed eggplant, deep fried small mackerel soaked in a sesame sauce, pork braised with beans, and congee with green peas appeared on the table. When I saw the servants helping mother boil the Chinese cabbage before soaking in great earthen jars, I knew that the short months of autumn would turn the cabbage into preserved greens for our traditional Chinese fire-kettle in the winter. The traditions in eating passed on for generations brought the feeling of togetherness in the family around that table. Mealtimes saw the family discussing and solving problems that otherwise would have gone unheeded. This family atmosphere with the flavor of these childhood dishes I shall carry with me always.

As the eldest grandchild in the Ma family, I was spoiled and pampered by grandparents, parents, and relatives alike. My husband, after our marriage, not only tolerated this but continued to spoil me to such an extent that he thought we should eat out rather than have me spend hours in the kitchen to cook. Also, whenever and whatever I cooked, he never complained. I am really grateful to him for his understanding, but, on the other hand, this made me into the worst cook in our family. Yet, due to our perpetual visits to famous restaurants around the world, I developed a discriminating palate, which did help me to cook much later.

I must admit that the fire for cooking that I must always have had was rekindled during the last three years. Since the birth of our son, it has become more difficult to go out as often. Also, our friends both in Europe and Japan, knowing of my mother's famous cookbooks, were highly dissappointed if I could not offer them a decent Chinese meal. This encouraged me to set my kitchen in order, of course always with one of mother's books propped in front of me, labeled by husband as my "Bible."

Since my husband is with Lufthansa, the German airline, his assignments took us more and more to countries where some of the ingredients for Chinese cooking were unattainable. This produced the beginning of my "space recipes," as he calls them, where I let fantasy run free. Sauerkraut was used instead of Chinese preserved cabbage; veal, tastier than beef in Europe, substituted for Kobe beef. The apple dessert here uses a fruit found almost anywhere in the world. Mango and papaya in tropic countries substituted for Chinese vegetables; pork roulade was inspired by Chinese spring rolls and European taste.

I do hope our readers will find as much enjoyment in these recipes as many of our friends. In all of them, I have not tried to break loose too far from orthodox Chinese flavor, but, by using the available ingredients in the West, have tried to bring a blending of East and West in cooking.

Chop, Chop, Chop, Stir, Stir, Tiddly Dum

 Helen Ma Yamawaki

The editor of this book is a cockroach. Always in and out of the kitchen when we were preparing for the photos. Nibble, nibble, nibble—and who needs all that advice? And he says to define what Chinese cooking is because my recipes are new and "creative." Really. I mean, it's simple. Chinese cooking is just Chinese cooking, which is anything. Almost. Even steak and mashed potatoes, if you put them together right, can be Chinese.

"Create"—this word seems to fit into any category. I like the way it sounds and you can use it as often as you wish, especially when something "new" hits your mind. I, myself, never dreamed of putting this word into my cooking. Neither did my mother— I believe; when she first handed her cookbook to me when I was to leave to Hawaii for school. Inside she wrote:

> To my dearest daughter Helen:
>> Be always healthy, happy and sweet as you are [which all mothers think of their daughters].
>> Cooking is universal friendship maker.
>>> Love,
>>> Mommy

The impact of the last sentence never hit me until I met a few friends who found out my mother was Mrs. Nancy Chih Ma herself, the famous author of the best selling Chinese cookbook. They started, "Oh, Helen, you must teach me some tricks of it. I HAVE your mother's COOKBOOK!" expecting *me* to be just the same as Mrs. Ma. This is how I actually started to look through Mrs. Ma's cookbook for the first time *carefully*. And did I try hard when a few days later I had my friends over for dinner? No; it was simple. I don't know if the book did it or Mrs. Ma's blood, which also runs in me, did it, but it was just like boiling an egg. And my friends are still my dearest friends even now.

And here Miss Creativity exits. She had omitted everything she did not like or whatever she could not find at home, or, rather, did not have time to go to Chinatown to look for. Instead she added whatever she liked or had in hand (leftovers, too!). For chopping, also, instead of mincing she chopped some chunks, but not too far off. She always remembered what something should taste like—if something is going to be called sweet and sour pork, it should TASTE like sweet and sour pork except that it might look a little different from the orthodox dish. Keep the taste in mind and a dish will be a pure Chinese dish. If anyone says that they don't know what Chinese food tastes like, I don't believe it. In that unlikely case, run, quick, to your local Chinese restaurant and have a feast—or, better yet, try out some of my mother's or Irene's recipes in this book. But sometimes, if you find yourself far off the mark in trying to make a new Chinese dish—and it is easy to go astray—just give the dish some new name.

In one of my recipes you will notice that I have stolen back the macaroni from the Italians, which, as a Chinese, I still believe that Marco Polo originally borrowed from China. I do hope no one will take this too seriously, because I believe cooking is not to be serious—it should be enjoyable, like putting on makeup and suddenly finding yourself beautiful. Maybe for the men this is like choosing and matching a new necktie with a new color shirt.

I am so proud to present this book here, for not many families can put themselves together and present something as one. And I want to thank my mother dearly, in much more than these few words here. She has put all this into me and taught me to love friends and cooking. If someday I shall be the mother of a daughter, I will do the same.

The Ma Family Chinese Cookbook

Hors d'Oeuvres of the North (p. 47): Sweet and Sour Spareribs (center); River Shrimp; Sweet and Sour Cucumbers; Chicken (top); Abalone (bottom); Crab; Pine Nuts; Raisins: Deep Fried Water Chestnut Chips (bottom left); Pumpkin Seeds; Peanuts; Apricots; Walnuts

21

Chinese Cabbage with Ham (p. 61); Fried Chicken with Peking Sauce (p. 114);
Prawns with Walnuts (p. 73)

Chicken and Chrysanthemums (p. 115); Paper-Wrapped Beef (p. 131); Shrimp with Asparagus (p. 72)

Braised Shark's Fins (p. 68); Cuttlefish with Peppers (p. 73); Egg Rolls (p. 104);
Szechwan Smoked Duck (p. 121)

Creamed Scallops (p. 74); Stuffed Duck (p. 122); Cloud Scroll Rolls (p. 105)

Piquant Pigs' Feet (p. 124); Chinese Pickles (p. 54)

Omelets with Spinach (p. 106); Flower Buns (p. 110); Fried Pork (p. 124)

Braised Lamb with Garlic (p. 123); Jade and Gold (p. 60); Chilled Noodles with
Spicy Sauce (p. 111)

Chicken in Yunnan Pot (p. 136); Chicken and Vegetables with Chili (p. 115); Sizzling Rice (p. 110)

Hors d'Oeuvres of the South (p. 49): *clockwise*, Steamed Lobster; Fried Crab Balls; Chilled Celery; Fried Shrimp Balls; Swatownese Braised Goose; Fried Fish Balls; Cuttlefish Rings

Chinese Beef Steak (p. 132); Stuffed Prawns (p. 74); Elegant Chicken (p. 116)

Swatownese Braised Goose and Garlic Sauce (p. 120); Swatownese Tea and Utensils
(see tea in Glossary)

Braised Beef with Eggs (p. 133); Abalone with Vegetables (p. 76); Sweet and Sour
Fish and Sauce (p. 70); Chicken Wine Soup (p. 138)

Sweet Pea Soup (p. 142); Sweet Taro with Gingko Nuts (p. 141); Sweet Bird's Nest with Quail Eggs (p. 142)

In What, With What, and How

The Kitchen

The two basic, irreplaceable tools of a Chinese kitchen are a very sharp knife and a frying pan. The best pan is the wok. These two utensils are the hammer and saw and brush and ink with which any cook can build culinary palaces filled with paintings and poetry.

Knives: Whatever kitchen knives you are accustomed to working with and that fit your hand well are fine. The important point is that any knife should be kept as sharp as possible at all times. This is absolutely necessary if you consider the amount of time and nervous energy saved when working with a sharp knife. Also, you can do more with a sharp knife, and foods taste better. Shape, juices, and patience are lost when you try to force a dull knife through ingredients.

A small Chinese cleaver (photo, page 40) is very much worth the investment. Again, if kept sharp, its versatility is amazing. Its weight allows chopping through bones, and it can be used even for fine shaving and cutting.

Stainless steel knives naturally are convenient, but take work to keep sharp. An ordinary tempered steel knife is kept free of rust by rubbing it occasionally with salad oil, drying it thoroughly, and wrapping the blade with wax paper between uses.

Chopping Board: For any kitchen, a small, raised chopping board with one end cut into a semicircle (photo, page 40) is ideal. It is a good height for easy work and also allows a wok, frying pan, or saucepan to be put under the board and the chopped ingredients to slipped directly into the pan without spilling or fuss. Unfortunately, these boards are not commercially available, but were made to order by Mrs. Ma for her Tokyo cooking classes. However, feel free to use this idea (or improve on it) and have your own chopping board made from a good hard wood. For those with large kitchens, a Chinese chopping board, which is a six-inch-thick section of hardwood tree trunk, is extremely handy. With a heavy chopping board and with a large amount of chopped ingredients, the trick is to slide a cleaver underneath the chopped food and transfer it on the cleaver to the pan.

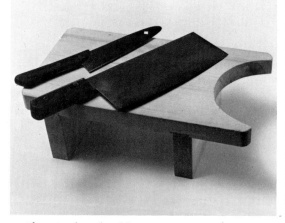

1. Chopping board and knives.

2. Wok, burner crown, strainer, ladle, and spatula.

Pots and Pans: The Chinese wok (photo, this page) cannot be overpraised. It is the best tool made for the job. The round surface distributes heat evenly and combines features of both frying pan and saucepan. For stir-frying, especially, a wok allows ample room and depth for vigorous action with either a large or small amount of ingredients. Pictured with the wok in the photo are a strainer for deep frying or parboiling, a ladle, and a spatula designed for the round surface. Under the wok is a burner crown, which can be used on either a gas or electric range.

If you do not have a wok (and if one is not available), a good, deep, and well-seasoned cast-iron or enameled frying pan may be used.

A Chinese bamboo steamer (photo, this page) is also well worth the investment. Besides, they are very attractive and add atmosphere to your kitchen if displayed well. All kinds of steamers can be improvised; perhaps the simplest is a bowl centered on a rack in a large covered pot or Dutch oven (the bowl should not touch the pot sides), with water about two inches below the bowl rim. Taking hot things out of such a

3. Steamer on conventional saucepan

4. Cutting methods: (left to right) top—cubing, dicing, shred-cutting, lengthwise slicing, wedging; bottom —crosswise slicing, diagonal slicing, fine chopping, shred-cutting (leek), scoring.

steamer is a bit bothersome. Not only is a Chinese bamboo steamer the most convenient, it can be stacked in two or more layers and allow several dishes to be steamed simultaneously. The steamer in the photo is set on a saucepan, but the wok is traditionally used as the steam source.

Preparing
The main reason these principles are being mentioned here is so you can break them. For most Chinese dishes, and especially for stir-frying, more time is spent over the cutting board than over the stove. There are really only three types of cutting—big, medium, and small—which are determined by the cooking method. That is, generally, small and medium sizes are for stir-frying, medium and large sizes are for braising. Steaming and deep frying can take any size. Refinements of shape and proportion of cut ingredients are determined by the nature of the food—whether tough, grained, soft, layered, etc.— and by the effect you want to achieve. A general rule is that all the ingredients for one

41

dish are cut to approximately the same size. But this has all kinds of exceptions. The photo on page 41 shows ten cutting variations; a glance at the photo and a few experiments and you can go ahead and ignore the cutting directions if you want.

Every Chinese cookbook seems to have its own cutting vocabulary. Following is a quick run-down of the words used here. Consistency has been avidly pursued, but there are some points that are controversial. Like how do you slice a turnip lengthwise?

Slicing: Where the type of slicing is not specified in the recipe, it means that anything goes. The one type of slicing that may be a little different is the diagonal (lower row, second from left), which means slicing at an angle to the axis of the ingredient. Wedging (upper row, right) is a variation used for harder ingredients in which a large surface area is exposed by cutting at different angles to form triangular chunks.

Shred-cutting: This is probably the most bothersome cutting technique, until you get the hang of it, but is basic to Chinese cooking, especially to stir-frying. The example in the photo (upper row, center) shows the most common shred-cut size; the leek segment in the lower row has been more finely shred-cut.

Dicing: Cutting across strips or shred-cut ingredient produces squares of desired size. To differentiate between sizes (upper row, left), the large may be called cubing and the small, dicing.

Fine Chopping: The example in the photo (lower row, center) was achieved by cutting across a finely shred-cut leek. Anything finer than this is referred to here as mincing. When recipes just state "chopped" without further clarification, you have your choice.

Scoring: Cuttlefish and liver stir-fry well if first deeply scored in a crisscross pattern (lower row, right) before being cut into the appropriate-sized pieces.

Cooking

The one unbreakable principle of Chinese cooking is that food should be as fresh as possible. All foods, whether whole or cut small, should be cooked fast and hot—as fast and hot as possible. Soggy gray vegetables or meats do not exist in Chinese cooking.

5. Vegetables: (left to right) Chinese cabbage, taro, lotus root, bean sprouts, leek.

Stir-frying: This involves nothing more than stirring ingredients vigorously (if not too delicate) in a little oil over high heat. Heat the dry pan first, add oil, heat until it roils, add ingredients, and go! The order of ingredients added varies according to their delicacy and cooking time, but usually the order (after the oil) is: solid seasonings like ginger, leek, and chili pepper; meat; salt and liquid seasonings; vegetables; additional liquid or stock, if called for; and cornstarch mixture. Unless otherwise specified here, stir-frying should always be done over high heat. A large frying pan gives ample room for heating all ingredients; always give yourself ample room—trying to stir-fry in a six-

6. Dried and Canned Ingredients: (left to right) dried Chinese mushrooms, dried cloud ear mushrooms, shark's fin, water chestnuts, gingko nuts, bamboo shoots (large and small), baby corn, transparent vermicelli.

inch pan is a lost cause. With a wok, however, there will be no worry about pitching food out of the pan.

One important time and nerve saver is to prepare all cut ingredients and mix all seasonings and cornstarch-water mixtures ahead of time. In fact, two or more stir-fried dishes served at one meal are impossible without advance preparation. Then it is a snap.

Deep Frying: There is some variation in the deep frying temperatures in this book. For meats and anything else that is not delicate, hot (360°) oil is the rule. Delicate batters, some vegetables, and other items take lower temperatures. Deep frying should be done as fast as possible at the highest temperature tolerance of a particular ingredient. A little bit of experimentation will determine the best temperature for any ingredient not mentioned here. Remember that food continues to cook for a bit after taken out of the oil.

Steaming: Occasionally in the recipes, "steam over high heat" is recommended. Unless otherwise specified, high heat is the rule. Also, like an oven, a steamer should be preheated before putting in food. In fact, a steamer can be considered a wet-atmosphere oven in practice. Dry-atmosphere cooking (baking, roasting) seems to be largely a Western technique. Unlike an oven, however, turn off the heat, remove the lid from the steamer, and let the heat disperse briefly before removing the cooked food.

Thinking about Ingredients

The main ingredients are all defined and discussed in the Glossary, but a little mulling over ifs and how-tos seems appropriate here.

Oil: It seems that American aversion to fried foods is just beginning to disappear with the appearance of good, light vegetable oils on the market. China has been fortunate in having excellent oils, and Chinese cooking has evolved with and around the successful use of oil. Any light vegetable oil that does not burn with high heat can be used, but safflower, corn, peanut, and cottonseed oils are usually preferred. Do not use olive oil or animal fats, butter, or any oil that solidifies at room temperature, unless specifically called for in the recipe for a special purpose. Cooking with vegetable oil over high heat immediately seals the surface of food, minimizes the loss of temperature-fragile vitamins, and allows a full, but light and nutritious meal. In short, Chinese food is healthy. What better praise? Used oil can be reused if $\frac{1}{2}$ leek and 4-5 slices ginger are first browned in it.

Soy Sauce: Some of the liquids marketed as soy sauce in the U.S. are better as seasonings for Western food than for use in Chinese cooking. Some of these are made from burnt sugar or by chemical process, are rather salty and bitter, and should be used as a last resort in the kitchen only when heavily diluted. The Kikkoman people in Japan have been marketing their soy sauce abroad for some years now. It should be on the shelves of most American markets and is completely dependable. If not available, it can be ordered. Since soy sauce is used like salt, purchase of a large can can be a practical economy. A handy kitchen bottle and a decorative table dispenser are also useful. You might also find the lighter grade of soy sauce (Japanese: *usukuchi shōyu*) pleasant both for cooking and as a seasoning.

Vegetables: In Japan, where this book was written, vegetables are generally smaller and more tender than in the United States and Europe. Also, the quality of vegetables seems to vary somewhat according to area in other countries. The authors have tried to keep this in mind, but all differences could not be taken into account. As a rule, then, choose the youngest and most tender vegetables, especially greens. If there is an Oriental grocer convenient, depend on him. Even so, it may be necessary to first parboil, slightly extend the cooking time of, or in some way slightly alter the directions for some vegetables indicated here, to compensate for differences in size and tenderness. Also, feel free to substitute any local, tender vegetables that you think appropriate. For instance, thinly sliced zucchini may be parboiled and stir-fried in a variety of combinations with great success.

Wine: Dry sherry is called for in these recipes, but this is a somewhat expensive substitute for Chinese rice wine. Since the Chinese wine is generally unavailable, Japanese saké, especially the drier varieties, is an excellent substitute. Saké is inexpensive and available almost anywhere now. If your neighborhood liquor store does not stock it, it should be easy to order. The only reason saké was not specified in the recipes was because of its lingering exotic associations and the fact that dry sherry, though expensive, is much more familiar. But beware—cooking sherry and cream sherry are not good substitutes. If your stock of saké or dry sherry runs out, try gin, light white rum, or any dry white distilled liquor.

Hors d'Oeuvres

❦ Hors d'Oeuvres
of the North

北方冷盤

COLOR: PAGE 21

RIVER SHRIMP

1 lb. river shrimp (or small shrimp)
5 Tbsps. oil
¼ tsp salt
1 Tbsp. dry sherry

Heat oil and stir-fry shrimp until color changes. Drain and sprinkle with salt and sherry to taste. Serves 6–8 as an hors d'oeuvre.

Note: River shrimp should not be shelled. Conventional shrimp may be shelled or left unshelled, as desired.

SWEET AND SOUR CUCUMBERS

5 cucumbers, washed, cut into 2-in. lengths, quartered
  lengthwise, and seeded
2 Tbsps. oil
2 small red chili peppers, seeded and shred-cut
SEASONINGS
  1 tsp. soy sauce
  2 Tbsps. sugar
  ½ tsp. salt
1 Tbsp. vinegar

Heat oil, add chili pepper, and stir-fry 3–4 seconds. Add cucumber, stir-fry 30 seconds, add SEASONINGS, and stir 3–4 times. Cool and refrigerate with liquid. Remove cucumbers from liquid and sprinkle with vinegar before serving. Serve chilled. Serves 6–8 as an hors d'oeuvre.

CHICKEN

Use sliced Silver Chicken (see recipe, p. 118)
SAUCE
    1 Tbsp. soy sauce
    ½ tsp. roughly ground anise pepper (or black pepper)
    1 Tbsp. sherry
    ½ tsp. salt

Pour SAUCE over sliced chicken and serve at room temperature. Meat of ½ chicken serves 4–6 as an hors d'oeuvre.

ABALONE

canned abalone, drained and out into bite-sized slices
SAUCE
    1 tsp. grated ginger
    1 Tbsp. dry sherry
    1 Tbsp. soy sauce

Pour SAUCE over abalone.

SWEET AND SOUR SPARERIBS

1½ lbs. spareribs, cut into 1-in. pieces
MARINADE
    1 Tbsp. dry sherry
    1 Tbsp. soy sauce
    1 tsp. ginger juice
1 Tbsp. cornstarch
oil for deep frying
SEASONINGS
    1 Tbsp. dry sherry
    2 Tbsps. sugar
    2 Tbsps. soy sauce
    1 Tbsp. vinegar
    ½ tsp. salt
1 tsp. cornstarch
1 Tbsp. sesame oil
1 Tbsp. finely chopped leek
1 Tbsp. finely chopped ginger

Mix marinade and marinate spareribs 20 minutes. Add cornstarch and mix until spareribs are coated. Heat oil and deep fry spareribs over medium heat 10 minutes. Drain. Mix SEASONINGS and cornstarch and set aside. Heat sesame oil, add leek and ginger, and stir-fry a few seconds. Add SEASONINGS mixture, stir constantly until thickened, add fried spareribs, and stir. Serve hot. Serves 3–4 as a main course. Serves 6–8 Chinese style or as an hors d'oeuvre.

canned crab, drained, cartilage removed, and broken
  into bite-sized pieces
pine nuts
raisins
sliced water chestnuts, deep fried and lightly salted
pumpkin seeds
peanuts
dried apricots
walnuts

Place sweet and sour spareribs in center of large
platter. Arrange other hors d'oeuvres around it and
garnish as desired.

🦐 Hors d'Oeuvres of the South   南方冷盤

COLOR: PAGE 30

Braised Swatownese Goose, sliced (see recipe, page
120).

STEAMED LOBSTER

1 small lobster, washed well
SOUR PLUM SAUCE
  2 large Chinese preserved plums or Japanese
    umeboshi (not dried)
  $\frac{1}{4}$ cup water
  4 tsps. sugar
  $\frac{1}{2}$ tsp. cornstarch mixed with 3 Tbsps. water

Place lobster on plate, put in preheated steamer and
steam for 20 minutes. Remove and cool. Remove
meat from shell and slice into bite-sized pieces. Arrange on serving plate. Remove plum pits and mash
meat through strainer. Place sieved plum, water, and
sugar in small saucepan and place over low heat,
adding cornstarch mixture slowly. Stir constantly
until thickened. Cool and serve as dip with lobster
Serves 4 as an hors d'oeuvre or Chinese style.

Note: Lobster shell may be reserved to be used as
decoration on hors d'oeuvres serving plate.

FRIED FISH BALLS

$\frac{3}{4}$ lb. white meat fish fillet, minced and ground to fine paste in mortar
$\frac{1}{4}$ cup water
3 tsps. dry sherry
$\frac{3}{4}$ tsp. salt
$\frac{1}{2}$ tsp. white pepper
$1\frac{1}{2}$ tsps. oil
1 tsp. cornstarch
oil for deep frying

Mix all ingredients except oil for deep frying, and form into small balls 1 inch in diameter. Bring ample water to boil and drop in fish balls a few at a time. When they float on the surface, remove and drain. Pat dry with kitchen paper. Heat oil to hot (360°) and deep fry until light brown. Drain on absorbent paper. Serve hot with catsup as dip. Makes about 15 balls.

FRIED CUTTLEFISH RINGS

2 medium cuttlefish, cleaned and intestines, thin skin, head, and feet removed without cutting body
MARINADE
    1 Tbsp. dry sherry
    2 tsps. ginger juice
    $\frac{1}{2}$ tsp. salt
    dash white pepper
oil for deep frying

Slice cuttlefish into $\frac{1}{4}$-inch-thick rings and cut tentacles into $1\frac{1}{2}$-in. lengths. Mix MARINADE and marinate cuttlefish 5 minutes. Heat oil to medium (340°) and deep fry cuttlefish 5–8 minutes, then drain on absorbent paper. Serve hot with catsup as dip. Serves 5–6 as an hors d'oeuvre or Chinese style.

CHILLED CELERY

SAUCE
    2 Tbsps. sugar
    4 Tbsps. hot water
    8 Tbsps. fish sauce (or soy sauce)
    4 Tbsps. ice water
    $\frac{1}{2}$ tsp. sesame oil
1 lb. celery (about 8 stalks), halved lengthwise, each half cut into $1\frac{1}{2}$-in. lengths
2 Tbsps. dried small shrimp, soaked in water until slightly soft

Dissolve sugar in hot water; add fish sauce (or soy sauce), ice water, and sesame oil, and stir well. Place celery and dried shrimp in deep bowl, add sauce, and refrigerate 3–4 hours. Serve chilled. Serves 5–6 as an appetizer or Chinese style.

Note: If celery is to be kept overnight, add $\frac{1}{2}$ cup more water.

Fried Crab Balls

SWEET PLUM SAUCE

- 1 Tbsp. plum jam (or preserves)
- ¼ cup water
- ¼ tsp. vinegar
- 3 drops soy sauce
- ½ tsp. cornstarch mixed with 1 Tbsp. water

CRAB BALLS

- 1 cup canned crabmeat, cartilage removed and broken into shreds
- 2 tsps. dry sherry
- ¼ tsp. grated ginger
- ¼ tsp. salt
- dash white pepper
- 1 Tbsp. chopped pork fat (or shortening; but not butter)
- 2 canned water chestnuts, chopped finely
- oil for deep frying

Mix plum jam with about ½ tsp. water (mash through strainer if plum preserves are used). Add vinegar, soy sauce, and remaining water. Place mixture in small saucepan over low heat and add cornstarch mixture slowly, stirring constantly until thickened. Cool. Mix all ingredients for crab balls well and shape into walnut-sized balls. Heat oil to hot (360°) and deep fry balls until golden brown. Drain on absorbent paper and serve hot with sauce as dip. Makes about 15 balls.

Fried Shrimp Balls

- 1 lb. shrimp, shelled, deveined, and finely chopped
- 1 Tbsp. dry sherry
- ½ tsp. ginger juice
- ¼ tsp. salt
- ½ tsp. cornstarch
- 1 Tbsp. finely chopped pork fat (or shortening; but not butter)
- 1 tsp. finely chopped parsley
- dash white pepper
- oil for deep frying

Mix all ingredients except oil, and shape into walnut-sized balls. Heat oil to hot (360°) and deep fry shrimp balls until golden brown. Drain on absorbent paper. Serve hot with catsup or sweet plum sauce (see recipe, left) as dip. Makes about 12 balls.

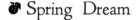

🌸 Spring Dream   春 夢

COLOR: page 90

$\frac{1}{2}$ lb. raw white meat fish or chicken filet, minced
very finely and ground to a fine paste in a mortar
with 1–2 Tbsps. water

SEASONINGS

$\frac{1}{2}$ tsp. ginger juice
$\frac{1}{2}$ egg white
$\frac{1}{2}$ tsp. salt
1 tsp. dry sherry
1 Tbsp. cornstarch

3–4 slices boiled ham, cut into 1$\frac{1}{2}$ x 2-in. rectangles
1 hard-boiled egg yolk, crumbled finely

Mix fish (or chicken) paste with SEASONINGS until
smooth. Cut paper cherry blossom petal shape from
clean white paper (see process photo, p. 103), about
2 inches long, place pattern on 2–3 ham rectangles,
and cut petal shapes. Place about 1 Tbsp. paste mixture in a footed Japanese saké cup (see photo), a small
aluminum foil cup about $\frac{2}{3}$ thumb-length deep (foil
cup should be lightly oiled), or any heatproof cup of
approximately the same size. Insert bottoms of five
ham petals into paste mixture around circumference
of cup, place cups in steamer, and steam over high
heat 20 minutes. Place dab of egg yolk in center of
each "blossom." Serve hot or at room temperature
as an hors d'oeuvre. Makes 15–20 "blossoms," de-
pending on size of cup.

Note: Cherry blossoms are not a prerequisite for this
dish. Any other decorative ideas can be easily adapted.

🌸 Dragon Pearls   龍 戲 球

COLOR: PAGE 93

5 slices bacon, halved
10 canned water chestnuts
oil for deep frying

Wrap each chestnut with bacon and secure with
toothpick. Heat oil to medium (340°) and deep fry
until bacon is slightly crisp. Drain. The bacon will
become crisper when removed from oil. Serve hot
as an hors d'oeuvre.

🦀 Crisp Crab Rolls   脆皮蟹卷

COLOR: PAGE 91

WRAPPINGS

    1 cup all-purpose flour, sifted with ½ tsp. salt

    1 egg, beaten lightly

    2–3 Tbsps. water

FILLING

    2 Tbsps. cream cheese

    1 green onion, minced

    1 can crabmeat, cartilage removed and broken into shreds

    ½ tsp. salt

oil for deep frying

Mix WRAPPING ingredients and knead dough on a lightly floured board until smooth. Place dough in a bowl, cover with damp cloth, and let stand 15 minutes. Roll out on a lightly floured board into ⅛-inch thickness (about like ravioli wrapping) and cut into 3-inch squares. (It might be more convenient to work with only half the dough at one time.) Mix FILLING ingredients and place 1 tsp. filling mixture in center of each wrapping. Roll like a spring roll (see process photos, p. 102), using only water to seal. Heat oil to medium (340°) and deep fry rolls until golden brown. Serve hot or at room temperature. Makes 20–22 rolls.

🐑 Jellied Lamb   羊 糕

1 lb. lean lamb, thinly sliced and parboiled

6 cups water

SEASONINGS

    1 leek, cut into 3-in. lengths

    4 slices ginger

    2 Tbsps. soy sauce

    1 clove garlic, crushed

    3 Tbsps. dry sherry

    2 tsps. sugar

    1 or 2 red chili peppers

2 Tbsps. unflavored gelatin mixed with 4 Tbsps. water

Place lamb in saucepan with water and bring to boil. Add SEASONINGS, bring to boil again, reduce heat to medium, and simmer (uncovered) until tender (about 20–30 minutes). The broth will boil down to about 2 cups. Separate lamb slices and arrange in deep bowl or aspic mold. Strain broth through cheesecloth and discard solid seasonings. Add gelatin mixture to hot liquid (heat again if it has cooled) and stir until gelatin is completely dissolved. Pour gelatin liquid over lamb slices and refrigerate until set. Slice and serve. Serves 10 as an hors d'oeuvre or Chinese style.

Salads

🍎 Chinese Pickles 泡菜

COLOR: PAGE 26

4 green peppers, cut into bite-sized pieces
½ head cabbage, cut into bite-sized pieces
4 pickling cucumbers, sliced into ¼ × 2-in. strips
4 small turnips, sliced
4 small carrots, sliced lengthwise and cut into leaf shapes
4 stalks celery, cut into 2-in. lengths
1 stalk leek, cut diagonally into 2-in. lengths.
1 head lettuce, leaves separated, and torn into bite-sized pieces
15 cups water

SEASONINGS
    6 slices ginger
    10 small red chili peppers
    2 tsps. black peppercorns
    ¼ lb. salt
    2 Tbsps. dry sherry

Wipe vegatables with cloth and dry 6–8 hours. Bring water to boil, add SEASONINGS, immediately remove from heat, and cool. Place vegetables in a large glass jar or crock and pour seasoned brine over them to cover. The pickled vegetables may be served the next day in summertime, but should be allowed to stand 3 or 4 days in other seasons. Serves 15.

Note: Vegetables should be washed well before cutting. Pickled vegetables should be removed from liquid with clean chopsticks or similar instruments to prevent crushing. As vegetables are used, more may be added to the brine, in which case, 1 tsp. salt, $\frac{1}{2}$ cup dry sherry, and 1 Tbsp. brown sugar should be added to brine at the same time. The container shown in the color picture is a special Chinese pickle jar. By pouring water around the cover, air is prevented from entering the jar.

❧ Lettuce Salad   拌 生 菜

$\frac{1}{2}$ head lettuce, leaves separated and torn into 3-in. shreds
$\frac{1}{4}$ lb. boiled chicken, roughly shredded
2 slices boiled ham, shred-cut
DRESSING
    1 Tbsp. soy sauce
    3 Tbsps. vinegar
    1 tsp. mustard
    2 Tbsps. sesame oil
    3–4 green onions, chopped finely
    1 tsp. finely chopped fermented black beans (or anchovies)

Combine lettuce, chicken, and ham. Mix DRESSING, pour over salad, and toss. Serves 2–3 as a salad course. Serves 4–6 Chinese style.

❧ Dried Preserved Turnips   萝 蔔 乾

$2\frac{1}{2}$ lbs. turnips, quartered vertically
$3\frac{1}{3}$ oz. salt
$1\frac{3}{4}$ oz. salt

Dredge turnips with $3\frac{1}{3}$ oz. salt and dry in strong sunshine 5–6 hours. Mix well with $1\frac{3}{4}$ oz. salt with hands for about 10 minutes. Store in air-tight jar two days. Moisture will appear during this storage time. Again dry in sunshine for two days. Store in an air-tight jar. Turnips will shrink $\frac{1}{2}$ to $\frac{2}{3}$ original weight.

❧ Turnip Tidbit   乾 萝 蔔

$\frac{1}{2}$ lb. dried preserved turnips, cut into $1 \times \frac{1}{2} \times \frac{1}{4}$-in. pieces
$1\frac{3}{4}$ tsps. sugar
$3\frac{3}{4}$ tsps. grated brown ginger (or 2 tsps. grated regular ginger, dried in sun 2 hours)
$2\frac{3}{4}$ tsps. Mei-kwei-chiu liquor (or $1\frac{1}{4}$ tsps. brandy)

Mix turnips with sugar and brown ginger. Add liquor and mix well. Remove to serving plate and serve as cocktail snack or side dish for a meal. Serves 6–8.

❀ Papaya and Celery Salad 拌芹菜

COLOR: PAGE 84

2 stalks celery, cut into ½-in. pieces
½ tsp. salt
1 papaya (fresh or frozen), peeled, halved, and seeded
2 Tbsps. vinegar
½ tsp. Tabasco sauce
pinch salt

Sprinkle celery with salt, and place in cavities of papaya halves. Mix vinegar, Tabasco, and salt, and pour over celery. Serve chilled. Serves 2 as a salad course. Serves 4–6 Chinese style.

Note: Papaya can be diced and mixed with celery. One Tbsp. chopped peanuts or slivered blanched almonds may be added.

❀ Mango and Cabbage Salad 拌凉菜

COLOR: PAGE 86

½ lb. mangoes (fresh or frozen), peeled and shred-cut
½ lb. red cabbage, washed, cored, and shred-cut
½ tsp. salt

Sprinkle cabbage with salt and let stand 30 minutes. Mix mangoes with cabbage. Serve chilled. Serves 4 as a salad course. Serves 5–6 Chinese style.

Note: Sprinkle with sesame seeds and top with French dressing if desired.

❀ Cuttlefish and Celery Salad 魷魚芹菜

1 small cuttlefish, slit, head, legs and thin skin removed
2 stalks celery, stringed and cut into ½ × 3-in. sticks
SEASONINGS
    2 Tbsps. vinegar
    2 Tbsps. chicken stock
    1 Tbsp. soy sauce
    1 Tbsp. sesame oil

Boil cuttlefish until tender and milky white (about 10 minutes). Cool and cut into ½ × 3-inch strips. Mix SEASONINGS with cuttlefish and celery. Serve chilled. Serves 2 as a salad course. Serves 4 Chinese style.

🍅 Vegetables and Vegetables　蔬菜大會

COLOR: PAGE 92

broccoli flowerets, parboiled and crisped
celery, cut into sticks
canned baby corn
cucumber, cut into sticks
cherry tomatoes
DIP
 2 Tbsps. sesame paste (or peanut butter)
 $\frac{1}{2}$ Tbsp. vinegar
 $\frac{1}{2}$ tsp. sugar
 1 Tbsp. soy sauce
 1 Tbsp. sour cream

Mix DIP ingredients until smooth and arrange with vegetables on platter. Any other fresh, crisp vegetables such as carrots, turnips, cauliflower, etc. may be used.

🍅 Jellied Chicken　鷄凍

COLOR: PAGE 95

1 lb. chicken filet
SEASONINGS
 1 tsp. dry sherry
 1 leek, cut into 2-in. lengths
 5 slices ginger
 $\frac{1}{2}$ tsp. salt
 5–6 black peppercorns
2 Tbsps. unflavored gelatin
1 cucumber, shred-cut
1 radish, sliced thinly

Place chicken and SEASONINGS in saucepan, add water to cover, cover pan, and boil over high heat 10 minutes. Remove chicken and set aside. Strain 2 cups liquid through cheesecloth and discard ginger, peppercorns, leek, and remaining liquid. Place 2 cups strained chicken liquid in saucepan, add gelatin, and stir over low heat until dissolved. Shred chicken, add to gelatin mixture, and add cucumber and radish. Pour into bowl or aspic mold and chill until set. Serves 2–3 as a salad course. Serves 4–5 Chinese style.

Tomato Towers 紅柿塔

COLOR: PAGE 96

1 cup canned chicken, cubed
3 Tbsps. minced onion
½ cup chicken stock
2 Tbsps. sesame paste (or peanut butter)
1 Tbsp. chili sauce
1 Tbsp. sugar
½ tsp. salt
½ Tbsp. sesame oil
4 tomatoes, each cut horizontally into 3 slices
2 leaves lettuce, torn into 2-in. squares

Mix all ingredients except tomatoes and lettuce. Stuff lettuce and chicken mixture between tomato slices and fasten with toothpick. Garnish with parsley or olives. Serve chilled. Serves 4 as a salad course. Serves 8 Chinese style.

Beef Salad Rolls 牛肉卷

10 thin slices roast beef
3 stalks celery, stringed and cut into thin 3-in. lengths
3 cucumbers, seeded and cut into thin 3-in. lengths
1 leek, cut into 3-in. shreds
DIP A
    2 Tbsps. mild prepared mustard
    2 Tbsps. chicken stock
    1 Tbsp. bean paste
DIP B
    1 Tbsp. sesame paste (or peanut butter)
    2 Tbsps. soup stock
    2 tsps. soy sauce
    1 tsp. grated garlic

Arrange beef slices and vegetables on serving plate. Mix DIPS A and B. Serve at room temperature. Roll vegetables as desired in beef slices and dip before eating. Serves 2 as a salad course. Serves 5–6 Chinese style.

Note: Shred-cut green pepper and carrots also may be used if desired.

Beancurd with Zest　豆腐鹹菜

COLOR: PAGE 97

1 loaf beancurd, cut into 1 × 1 × 2-in. rectangles,
   then cut across longest diagonal
3 slices boiled ham, minced
2 dill pickles, minced (half-done Kosher dills recommended)

SEASONINGS
   2 Tbsps. soy sauce
   1 Tbsp. vinegar
   1 Tbsp. sesame oil
   dash pepper
1 small dill pickle, sliced lengthwise

Arrange beancurd on serving plate. Mix ham and
pickles with SEASONINGS and pour over beancurd.
Garnish with pickle slices. Serve at room temperature.
Serves 2–3 as a salad or appetizer. Serves 4 Chinese
style.

Vegetables

☙ Jade and Gold

燴 什 錦

COLOR: PAGE 28

4 Tbsps. oil
$\frac{3}{4}$ cup canned bamboo shoots, sliced lengthwise into
    bite-sized pieces
2–3 Chinese mushrooms, soaked in lukewarm water
    until tender, stemmed, and cut into bite-sized pieces
1 head brocolli, parboiled and flowerets separated
1 medium carrot, wedge-cut into bite-sized pieces
    and boiled until barely tender
8 canned water chestnuts
8 ears canned baby corn
6 champignons
$\frac{1}{4}$ cup canned gingko nuts
SEASONINGS
    1$\frac{1}{2}$ tsps. salt
    $\frac{1}{2}$ tsp. sugar
    1 Tbsp. dry sherry
    dash pepper
2 cups chicken stock
1 Tbsp. cornstarch mixed with 3 Tbsps. water

Heat oil, add all vegetables, and stir-fry over high
heat until coated with oil. Add SEASONINGS and stock.
Reduce heat to low and simmer 2 minutes. Add cornstarch mixture and stir until thickened. Serve hot.
Serves 3–4 as a vegetable course. Serves 5–6 Chinese
style.

Chinese Cabbage with Ham 火腿白菜

COLOR: PAGE 22

1 lb. Chinese cabbage, cut into 2 × 5-in. pieces
2 Tbsps. oil
1 cup chicken stock
4 slices boiled ham, edges notched decoratively and halved
½ cup milk
1 tsp. salt
2 tsps. cornstarch mixed with 2 Tbsps. water

Heat oil and stir-fry Chinese cabbage until coated with oil. Add stock and simmer over medium heat until Chinese cabbage is tender (about 5–10 minutes). Add ham, milk, salt, and cornstarch mixture and stir until thickened. Arrange Chinese cabbage on serving plate with ham on top. Serve hot. Serves 2–3 as a vegetable course. Serves 4–5 Chinese style.

Stuffed Lotus 炸藕塞肉

1 lb. lotus root, skinned and cut into ½-in. slices
1 Tbsp. vinegar mixed with 1 cup water
½ lb. ground beef or pork
SEASONINGS
  2 Tbsps. finely chopped leek
  1 tsp. ginger juice
  ½ tsp. salt
  1 Tbsp. soy sauce
BATTER
  2 eggs, beaten lightly
  ½ cup all-purpose flour
  ½ tsp. salt
oil for deep frying

Soak lotus root slices in vinegar water 10 minutes. Drain. Combine meat and SEASONINGS and mix well. Mix BATTER until smooth. Coat one lotus root slice with generous amount of meat mixture, top with another lotus slice, and squeeze lightly until meat filling comes up into holes of lotus and slices are firm. Repeat for all lotus slices. Heat oil to medium (340°), dip stuffed lotus into batter, and deep fry until golden brown. Serves 2–3 as a main course. Serves 6–8 Chinese style or as an hors d'oeuvre.

🔸 Braised Assorted Vegetables   燴 素 菜

COLOR: PAGE 33

½ head Chinese cabbage (about 1 lb.) (or Chinese *bok choy* greens), leaves halved
½ lb. mustard greens, leaves halved
8–10 dried Chinese mushrooms, soaked in lukewarm water until tender and stemmed
2 Tbsps. oil
½ tsp. salt
dash white pepper
½ cup soup stock

Heat oil in deep saucepan, and stir-fry Chinese cabbage, mustard greens, and mushrooms briefly until coated with oil. Add salt, white pepper, and soup stock, bring to boil over high heat, reduce heat to medium, cover, and simmer 20 minutes, turning vegetables once. Arrange cabbage and greens on serving dish with mushrooms on top, and pour liquid over them. Serve hot. Serves 3–4 as a vegetable course. Serves 6–8 Chinese style.

🔸 Crabmeat Creamed Chinese Cabbage   蟹肉燴白菜

COLOR: PAGE 36

1 head Chinese cabbage, halved lengthwise
5 cups chicken stock (or water)
½ tsp. salt
1 cup chicken stock
2 Tbsps. flour
dash pepper
pinch salt
½ cup evaporated milk
⅔ cup canned crabmeat, cartilage removed and broken into shreds
4 Tbsps. finely chopped ham

Place cabbage in deep saucepan with 5 cups stock and salt, bring to boil, cover, and simmer 20 minutes. Drain and arrange on serving plate. Mix 1 cup stock with flour in saucepan until smooth, add salt and pepper, and slowly stir in evaporated milk over medium heat. Cook, stirring constantly, until mixture begins to boil, add crabmeat, and pour over cabbage. Sprinkle with chopped ham and serve hot. Serves 4 as a vegetable course. Serves 6–8 Chinese style.

🌰 Stir-Fried Mixed Vegetables　　炒什錦素菜

2 Tbsps. oil
2 large Chinese mushrooms, soaked in lukewarm water until tender, stemmed, and shred-cut
1 green pepper, seeded and shred-cut
1 pimiento, seeded and shred-cut
1½ lbs. bean sprouts
½ tsp. salt
¼ tsp. dry sherry

Heat oil, stir-fry mushroom until coated with oil, add green pepper and pimiento, and stir-fry 30 seconds. Add bean sprouts, sprinkle with salt and sherry, and stir-fry 2–3 seconds. Serve hot. Serves 2–3 as a vegetable course. Serves 4–5 Chinese style.

🌰 Braised Broccoli　　燴西蘭菜

1 head broccoli, flowerets separated, stems skinned, and sliced into 2-in. lengths
3 Tbsps. oil
1 tsp. salt
1 tsp. sugar
1½ cups chicken stock (or water)
1 Tbsp. cornstarch mixed with 3 Tbsps. water
2 slices boiled ham, chopped finely

Parboil broccoli flowerets in salted water and drain. Heat oil, stir-fry broccoli 3–4 seconds, and add salt, sugar, and stock. When liquid boils, add cornstarch mixture, stirring constantly until thickened. Serve hot. Garnish with ham. Serves 2 as a vegetable course. Serves 4 Chinese style.

Note: Take care not to overcook broccoli.

🌰 Emerald Asparagus　　炸翡翠露笋

1 lb. fresh asparagus, hard stems removed and halved
BATTER
　　1 egg, beaten lightly
　　1 cup flour
　　½ tsp. baking powder
　　½ tsp. salt
　　dash pepper
　　½ cup water
oil for deep frying

Parboil asparagus in lightly salted water, plunge immediately into cold water (to preserve color) and leave just until cool. Mix BATTER. Heat oil to medium (340°). Dip each asparagus stalk into batter, leaving about ¾ inch uncoated, and deep fry immediately until batter is light yellow. Drain and serve hot. Serves 3 as a vegetable course. Serves 6–8 Chinese style.

❈ Three Sisters　　姉 妹 花
COLOR: PAGE 86

½ cup chicken stock (or water)
1 lb. canned white asparagus
1 cup canned mushrooms or champignons
1 Tbsp. oyster sauce
2 tsps. cornstarch mixed with 3 Tbsps. water
½ lb. spinach, washed, stemmed, and leaves halved
3 Tbsps. oil
pinch salt
SAUCE
    1 Tbsp. dry sherry
    1 cup chicken stock
    2 tsps. sesame oil
    1 Tbsp. cornstarch

Bring stock to boil in saucepan, reduce heat to low, and add asparagus, mushrooms, oyster sauce, and cornstarch mixture. Stir lightly until thickened. Remove to serving plate. Heat oil, add spinach and salt, and stir-fry about 2–3 minutes. Remove to serving plate. Mix SAUCE in saucepan and bring to boil over medium heat. Stir until thickened, then pour over vegetables. Serve hot or at room temperature. Serves 3 as a vegetable course. Serves 6 Chinese style.

Note: Soy sauce can be substituted for oyster sauce.

❈ Sauerkraut with Beef　　牛肉炒酸菜
COLOR: PAGE 88

½ lb. lean beef, shred-cut
MARINADE
    1 Tbsp. dry sherry
    2 tsps. soy sauce
    ½ tsp. cornstarch
7 Tbsps. oil
1½ cups sauerkraut, soaked in water 5 minutes and water squeezed out well
½ tsp. salt
¼ cup shaved almonds

Mix MARINADE and marinate beef 5 minutes. Heat oil and stir-fry beef until color changes. Add sauerkraut and salt and stir-fry 5 minutes longer. Remove to serving plate and top with shaved almonds. Serve hot. Serves 2 as a main course. Serves 4–5 Chinese style.

Note: In North China, a sour Chinese cabbage very similar to German sauerkraut is made in winter.

🌸 Cabbage with Apricots   炒卷心菜

COLOR: PAGE 87

1 lb. cabbage, washed, cored, and cut into bite-sized
   squares
3 Tbsps. oil
½ tsp. salt
1 cup canned apricots, drained

Heat oil, stir-fry cabbage until tender (about 2
minutes), add salt and apricots, and stir-fry 1 minute.
Serve hot or at room temperature. Serves 3–4 as a
vegetable course. Serves 5–6 Chinese style.

🌸 Phoenix Nest   炒素菜

COLOR: PAGE 88

3 Tbsps. oil
1 large carrot, shred-cut
2 green peppers, seeded and shred-cut
1 small onion, shred-cut
3 oz. transparent vermicelli, soaked in lukewarm
   water until soft, drained, and cut into 6-in. lengths
SEASONINGS
   1 Tbsp. dry sherry
   2 Tbsps. soy sauce
   ½ tsp. salt

   1 Tbsp. sugar
   1 Tbsp. vinegar

Heat oil and stir-fry carrot, green pepper, and onion
2–3 minutes. Add vermicelli and SEASONINGS and
stir-fry until all ingredients are well coated with
liquid. Serve hot or at room temperature. Serves 2–3
as a vegetable course. Serves 4–5 Chinese style.

🌸 Stuffed Green Peppers with   青椒塞蛋
Eggs and Crabmeat

5 medium green peppers, halved lengthwise and
   seeded
8 hardboiled eggs, shelled and chopped finely
¾ cup canned crabmeat, cartilage removed and broken into shreds
1 tsp. ginger juice
1 tsp. salt
2 Tbsps. sesame oil

Mix eggs, crabmeat, ginger juice, and salt. Stuff egg-
and-crabmeat mixture in cavities of green peppers.
Put stuffed green peppers in preheated steamer and
steam over high heat 15 minutes. Remove from
steamer, sprinkle with sesame oil, and serve hot or at
room temperature. Serves 3–4 as a main course.
Serves 8–10 Chinese style.

❧ Eggplant with Crabmeat　蟹粉茄子

5–6 small eggplants, skinned, and quartered lengthwise
oil for deep frying
2 Tbsps. oil
½ can crabmeat, cartilage removed and broken into
shreds
½ tsp. ginger juice
SEASONINGS
    ½ tsp. salt
    2 tsps. sugar
    2 tsps. bean paste mixed with 1 Tbsp. water
    1 Tbsp. dry sherry
    soy sauce to taste

Soak eggplant in water about 10 minutes. Drain and
pat dry. Heat oil to high (360°) and deep fry eggplants
until golden. Heat 2 Tbsps. oil, add crabmeat and
ginger juice, stir-fry until coated with oil, add eggplant and SEASONINGS, and cook 5 minutes more.
Serve hot. Serves 3 as a main course. Serves 6–7
Chinese style.

❧ Layered Cabbage　蒸千層白菜

COLOR: PAGE 93

½ head Chinese cabbage
FILLING
    ½ lb. ground pork
    3 Tbsps. minced green onion
    ½ tsp. ginger juice
    2 tsps. soy sauce
    1 tsp. cornstarch
SAUCE
    1 Tbsp. soy sauce
    1 Tbsp. vinegar
    2 Tbsps. sugar
    2 tsps. cornstarch
    1 cup liquid from steamed, filled cabbage

Steam or boil cabbage 10 minutes; discard liquid.
Mix FILLING and spread evenly and thinly between
cabbage leaves. Place cabbage in deep bowl and steam
until tender (about 20 minutes). Reserve one cup liquid. Mix SAUCE ingredients and heat in saucepan until
thickened, stirring constantly. Remove cabbage to
serving plate and pour sauce over it. Serve hot. Serves
4–5 as a main course. Serves 10–12 Chinese style.

Fish

❦ Steamed Fish with Beancurd　豆腐蒸魚

2 loaves beancurd, mashed
½ lb. white meat fish, chopped (either finely or
    roughly, as desired)
SEASONINGS
    1 tsp. ginger juice
    1 tsp. cornstarch
    1 Tbsp. dry sherry
    1 tsp. salt
    dash pepper
2 Tbsps. chopped leek
2 Tbsps. chopped parsley

Combine beancurd, fish, and SEASONINGS and mix
well. Place in bowl or casserole and steam 15 minutes.
Sprinkle with chopped leek and parsley and serve
hot. Serves 3–4 as a main course. Serves 8 Chinese
style.

🐟 Braised Shark's Fins 燴魚翅

COLOR: PAGE 24

3 small dried shark's fins

A

    3–4 cups thin chicken stock
    1 leek, cut into 2-in. lengths
    5 slices ginger
    4 Tbsps. dry sherry

B

    2 cups chicken stock
    3–4 Tbsps. chicken fat
    1 heart Chinese cabbage, parboiled and quartered

SEASONINGS

    3 Tbsps. dry sherry
    2 tsps. oyster sauce
    $\frac{1}{2}$ leek, cut into 2-in. lengths
    4 slices ginger
    $\frac{1}{2}$ tsp. salt
    1 Tbsp. sugar
    $\frac{1}{2}$ tsp. pepper
    $\frac{1}{4}$ cup Lao-chiu wine
1 Tbsp. cornstarch mixed with 3 Tbsps. water

PRELIMINARIES: Place shark's fins in large saucepan, cover with boiling water, bring to boil, remove from heat, and soak overnight. Fin fibers will swell, the length will shrink, and the width will increase during boiling. After soaking, scrape away skin in direction of fibers (from bone outward) with knife. Change water and bring to boil; cool and again scrape away remaining skin. Cut away bone and long and short fibers as indicated in diagram; discard bone but retain short fin fibers for other dishes. Again place in water and bring to boil. Fins may be kept for one week if brought to boil in a daily change of water.

TO BRAISE: Place softened fins in deep saucepan or frypan. Add A ingredients, bring to boil over medium heat, and boil until completely tender. Discard liquid. If a fishy smell remains, repeat process with A ingredients until smell disappears (1–2 times).

Heat chicken fat in deep frypan, add leek and ginger, and stir-fry until browned. Add stock, bring to boil, and discard leek and ginger. Add SEASONINGS, fins (taking care not to break), and parboiled Chinese cabbage heart. Boil over medium heat 10 minutes. Add cornstarch mixture and stir until thickened. Remove fins and cabbage to serving dish and top with liquid. Serve hot. Serves 3 as a main course. Serves 6–7 Chinese style.

Note: The short fin fibers should be cooked as described in PRELIMINARIES until tender, and may be added to soup, stir-fried dishes, and braised dishes as desired. Shark's fin combines well with crabmeat, crab eggs, and chicken.

Shark's fins are expensive, a challenge, and an adventure in cooking, but are one of China's most famous delicacies and well worth the effort. When a shark's fin course arrives during a Chinese banquet,

it is the custom to drink a toast to this delicate dish (and to the courage of the fisherman, the generosity of host and hostess, and the skill of the cook).

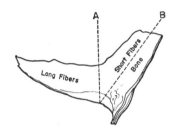

🐟 Baked Sesame Salmon 烤 魚

3 salmon steaks, cut into thirds
1 leek, shred-cut
1 green pepper, shred-cut
1 clove garlic, chopped
½ small red chili pepper, chopped
1 Tbsp. sesame seeds
2 Tbsps. soy sauce
2 tsps. vinegar
2 tsps. sugar
1 Tbsp. sesame oil
3 Tbsps. water

Combine all ingredients and let stand 30 minutes. Preheat oven to 400°. Wrap each piece of fish in foil and bake until tender (about 20 minutes). Serves 3 as a main course. Serves 7–9 Chinese style.

🐟 Steamed Pomfret 蒸 魚

COLOR: PAGE 35

1–1½ lb. pomfret (or any other white meat fish), scaled, cleaned, head and tail left intact
2 Tbsps. dry sherry
½ tsp. salt
dash white pepper
2 medium dried Chinese mushrooms, soaked in lukewarm water until tender, stemmed, and sliced into ⅛-in. strips
6–8 strips (⅛ × 1½-in.) pork fat
6 slices ginger, cut into strips
1 spring onion, cut into 1½-in. lengths
8 spring onions, boiled until just tender in salted water

Wash fish and pat dry. Make diagonal slits 1 in. apart in both directions to make a crisscross pattern. Sprinkle both sides of fish with sherry, salt, and pepper. Put on plate, and arrange mushroom, pork fat strips, ginger, and spring onion strips on top. Place in preheated steamer, and steam over high heat until done (about 15–20 minutes). Remove from steamer, arrange boiled spring onions around fish, and serve hot. Serves 2 as a main course. Serves 4–5 Chinese style.

❦ Sweet and Sour Fish Filet 糖醋魚

COLOR: PAGE 37

SAUCE
    ½ cup water
    1 tsp. cornstarch
    3 tsps. sugar
    1 tsp. vinegar
    ½ tsp. catsup
4 small white meat fish filets, cut diagonally into 2 or
   3 pieces
MARINADE
    2 Tbsps. dry sherry
    ¼ tsp. ginger juice
    1 tsp. salt
    2 tsps. cornstarch
1 egg beaten lightly
oil for deep frying

Put water and cornstarch in small saucepan and mix well. Place over low heat and add remaining SAUCE ingredients, stirring constantly until thickened. Pour into a sauce dish and set aside to cool. Mix MARINADE and marinate fish 15 minutes. Coat fish with egg. Heat oil to hot (360°) and deep fry fish until light brown. Drain on absorbent paper. Serve hot with sauce as dip. Serves 2 as a main course. Serves 4–5 Chinese style.

❦ Salmon with Soybeans 魚燉豆

COLOR: PAGE 85

1 cup dried soybeans
4 Tbsps. oil
6 salmon steaks
SEASONINGS
    1 onion, chopped finely
    4 slices ginger
    2 Tbsps. dry sherry
    3 Tbsps. soy sauce
    1 Tbsp. sugar

Soak beans overnight in ample water. Heat oil and fry salmon steaks to light brown on both sides. Add SEASONINGS, soybeans, and enough water to cover. Cover pan and simmer over low heat until tender (about 30 minutes). Serve hot or at room temperature. Serves 3 as a main course. Serves 6–8 Chinese style.

Note: This dish will keep for a week or more in refrigerator. The flavor of the beans will improve after a few days. Fresh, smoked, or salted salmon may be used.

❧ Crisp Fish with Pine Nuts 松子魚

COLOR: PAGE 87

oil for deep frying
¼ cup pine nuts
½ lbs. white meat fish, cleaned and scaled, head and tail left intact

SEASONINGS

   3 Tbsps. dry sherry
   dash pepper
   ½ tsp. salt
   1 Tbsp. cornstarch

SAUCE

   4 Tbsps. vinegar
   4 Tbsps. sugar
   ½ tsp. salt
   1½ Tbsps. cornstarch mixed with 1½ cups water
   2 Tbsps. catsup

Heat oil and deep fry pine nuts briefly, until golden brown, taking care not to scorch. Drain. Set aside. Make six or seven diagonal incisions to the bone along both sides of the fish. Mix SEASONINGS and rub on fish and into incisions. Heat oil (360°), gently slip fish into oil, and deep fry until golden brown. (Holding fish by the tail, dip the both sides into oil until the incisions are opened and the skin crispy. Then lower the whole fish into oil and fry another 15–20 minutes.) Drain and keep in a warm oven. Mix SAUCE and heat, mixing constantly until thickened. Pour sauce over the warm fish just before serving. Sprinkle with pine nuts. Serve hot. Serves 2–3 as a main course. Serves 4–6 Chinese style.

Note: Fish and sauce both can be prepared ahead. Heat fish in oven or refry for double crispness. Heat sauce in pan 15 minutes before serving.

❧ Fish with White Whiskers 刺蝟魚

COLOR: PAGE 97

½ lb. white meat fish filet, cut into 3 × 2-in. pieces

MARINADE

   2 Tbsps. dry sherry
   2 tsps. salt

cornstarch
1 egg white, beaten
1 cup transparent vermicelli, cut into ½-in. lengths
oil for deep frying

Mix fish and MARINADE and let stand 5 minutes. Dip each piece fish first in cornstarch (shake off excess cornstarch), then egg white, then vermicelli. Heat oil to medium (340°) and deep fry 2–3 fish pieces until vermicelli puffs up (about 1 minute). Remove immediately. Serve hot. Serves 2 as a main course. Serves 4 Chinese style.

Shellfish

🍤 Shrimp with Asparagus 炒蝦片露筍

COLOR: PAGE 23

½ lb. shrimp, shelled and deveined
MARINADE
    1 Tbsp. dry sherry
    1 small egg white
    1 Tbsp. cornstarch
    dash pepper
    pinch salt
¼ lb. (5–6 spears) green asparagus, hard stems removed
½ cup canned baby corn, cut into 1-in. lengths
5 Tbsps. oil
1 tsp. salt
½ tsp. sugar

Mix shrimp with MARINADE and let stand 5–10 minutes. Parboil asparagus in salted water, rinse in cold water, drain, and cut in 1-in. lengths. Heat oil and stir-fry shrimp just until color changes. Add asparagus, baby corn, salt, and sugar and stir-fry 30 seconds. Serve hot. Serves 2–3 as a main course. Serves 5–6 Chinese style.

🦐 Prawns with Walnuts　　炒蝦片

COLOR: PAGE 22

6 prawns, shelled, deveined, and each cut into 3 pieces
1 egg white
1 Tbsp. dry sherry
1 Tbsp. cornstarch
oil for deep frying
1 cup walnuts
4 Tbsps. oil
SEASONINGS
　　1 Tbsp. soy sauce
　　½ tsp. sugar
　　½ tsp. salt
1 Tbsp. vinegar

Mix prawns with egg white, sherry, and cornstarch. Heat oil to medium (340°) and deep fry walnuts until crisp. Walnuts scorch easily, so remove from oil as soon as color changes. Heat 4 Tbsps. oil, stir-fry prawns until color changes, and add SEASONINGS and deep fried walnuts. Stir-fry 1 minute. Serve hot. Serves 2 as a main course. Serves 4 Chinese style.

🦐 Cuttlefish with Peppers　　炒青椒魷魚

COLOR: PAGE 24

1 large cuttlefish, slit, cleaned, head, legs, and thin skin removed, scored in crisscross pattern on outside surface, and cut into bite-sized pieces
MARINADE
　　2 Tbsps. dry sherry
　　½ tsp. salt
　　2 Tbsps. cornstarch
2 cups green chili peppers (sweet)
4 Tbsps. oil
pinch salt
SEASONINGS
　　1 tsp. salt
　　1 tsp. vinegar
　　1 tsp. sugar

Mix MARINADE and marinate cuttlefish 10 minutes. Bring ample water to boil, add cuttlefish, and boil just until tender. Remove and drain. Slit side of each pepper and remove seeds. Heat oil, add pinch salt, and stir-fry peppers over high heat 1 minute. Add cuttlefish and SEASONINGS and stir-fry 30 seconds. Serve hot. Serves 2 as a main course. Serves 4 Chinese style.

● Creamed Scallops　　　　　奶油鮮貝

COLOR: PAGE 25

10 fresh scallops, skinned, and sliced into 2 or 3 pieces
2 Tbsps. dry sherry
1 Tbsp. cornstarch
4 Tbsps. oil
1 cup champignons
1 cucumber, peeled, seeded, cut into thin slices length-
　wise and diagonally into 1-in. lengths
SEASONINGS
　　1 tsp. salt
　　dash pepper
　　½ tsp. sugar
1 cup milk
1 tsp. cornstarch mixed with 1 Tbsp. water

Sprinkle scallops with sherry and cornstarch. Heat
oil and stir-fry scallops 1 minute. Add champignons
and cucumber, stir 2–3 times, add SEASONINGS and
milk, and bring to boil. Add cornstarch mixture,
stirring constantly until thickened. Serve hot. Serves
2 as a main course. Serves 4–5 Chinese style.

● Stuffed Prawns　　　　　炒大蝦

COLOR: PAGE 31

1 lb. small prawns, slit deeply down back and de-
　veined, leaving shell intact
6 cups water mixed with 4 tsps. salt
FILLING
　　4 Tbsps. finely chopped ginger
　　8 Tbsps. finely chopped spring onion (or green
　　　onion)
　　2 Tbsps. dry sherry
　　½ tsp. salt
　　dash pepper
3 Tbsps. oil

Soak prawns in salted water 10 minutes. Blot dry.
Mix FILLING and stuff prawns. Heat oil, carefully place
prawns, filling side down, in pan, and sauté about 2
minutes; then turn on sides and sauté both sides until
done (about 2 minutes). Serve hot. Serves 4 as a main
course. Serves 6–8 Chinese style.

🦐 Spicy Clams 燜蛤蜊

COLOR: PAGE 33

2 lbs. small clams
3 Tbsps. oil
2 1-in. cubes ginger, crushed
6 cloves garlic, chopped coarsely
1 small dried red chili pepper, seeded, sliced thinly
   into rings
2 Tbsps. dry sherry
½ tsp. salt
4 Tbsps. water

Soak clams in salted water for 2–4 hours with a clean iron nail (to remove sand). Heat oil, brown ginger and garlic; add chili pepper and stir-fry 1 minute. Add clams and stir fry over high heat 30 seconds. Add sherry, salt, and water, cover, and cook until shells open (about 2–3 minutes). Remove to serving plate and serve hot. Serves 2 as a main course. Serves 4–6 Chinese style.

Note: If large clams are used, cook covered until shells open (about 3–4 minutes). Clams that do not open have died and should be discarded.

🦐 Diamond Shrimp 炸大蝦

COLOR: PAGE 33

1 lb. medium shrimp
SEASONINGS
   4 tsps. dry sherry
   2 tsps. ginger juice
   1 tsp. salt
   ½ tsp. white pepper
   2 tsps. cornstarch
8–10 slices bread, crust removed and cut into ¼-in.
   cubes
oil for deep frying

Carefully shell ⅓ lb. shrimp, leaving tail and last shell segment intact. Deeply slit open backs, devein, and open out flat. Shell, devein, and finely chop remaining ⅔ lb. shrimp, and mix well with SEASONINGS. Divide shrimp mixture into same number of portions as number of opened shrimp. Heap chopped shrimp mixture generously on opened shrimp backs and also coat undersides. Cover shrimp mixture completely with bread cubes, pressing gently. Heat oil to medium (340°) and deep fry until golden brown. Serve hot with catsup as dip. Serves 4 as a main course. Serves 6–8 Chinese style or as an hors d'oeuvre.

🦀 Crab Sauté　　　　　　炒螃蟹

COLOR: PAGE 34

2 Tbsps. oil
$\frac{1}{4}$ cup shred-cut ginger
5 spring onions, cut into 2-in. lengths
1 large soft-shell crab, shelled, cleaned, meat cut into
　2-in. pieces, claws and shells cracked
SEASONINGS
　$\frac{1}{2}$ tsp. salt
　2 Tbsps. dry sherry
　$\frac{1}{2}$ tsp. sugar
　4 Tbsps. soup stock

Heat oil, stir-fry ginger quickly, add spring onion, and stir-fry 1 minute. Add crab, and stir-fry over high heat until color starts to change. Sprinkle with SEASONINGS, reduce heat to medium, cover, and cook 8 minutes. Serve hot. One large crab serves 2 as a main course. Serves 3–4 Chinese style.

Note: If canned soup stock or buillion is used, amount should be $1\frac{3}{4}$ Tbsps. soup stock and $2\frac{1}{4}$ Tbsps. water. Crab shell may be boiled until red and used in a decorative arrangement.

🦀 Abalone with Vegetables　什錦鮑魚片

COLOR: PAGE 37

$\frac{1}{2}$ cup liquid from canned abalone
dash white pepper
pinch salt
1 tsp. oyster sauce
1 tsp. sugar
1 Tbsp. cornstarch mixed with $\frac{1}{4}$ cup water
2 Tbsps. oil
6 slices ginger
$\frac{1}{2}$ cup canned small white mushrooms
$\frac{1}{2}$ cup canned baby corn
$\frac{1}{2}$ cup canned bamboo shoots, sliced thinly
10–12 carrot slices
1 can abalone, thinly sliced into bite-sized pieces

Mix abalone liquid, pepper, salt, oyster sauce, sugar, and cornstarch mixture and set aside. Heat oil, brown ginger, add mushrooms, baby corn, bamboo shoots, and carrot slices, and stir-fry 2 minutes. Add abalone and abalone juice mixture and stir until thickened (about 1 minute). Serve hot. Serves 2 as a main course. Serves 4–5 Chinese style.

☙ Seacliff Prawns

山裏紅大蝦

COLOR: PAGE 84

10 prawns, slit deeply down back with shell intact, deveined, and heads removed
5 Tbsps. oil
2 tsps. finely chopped ginger
3 Tbsps. finely chopped leek
SEASONINGS
    3 Tbsps. dry sherry
    1 Tbsp. sugar
    1 Tbsps. soy sauce
    2 Tbsps. catsup
    few drops Tabasco sauce
    ½ tsp. salt
2 tsps. cornstarch mixed with ½ cup water

Dip prawns in boiling water and set aside. Heat oil, add ginger and prawns, and stir-fry 2 minutes. Add chopped leek and SEASONINGS and stir-fry 30 seconds. Add cornstarch mixture and stir until thickened. Serve hot. Serves 2 as a main course. Serves 4–6 Chinese style.

Note: Tabasco may be omitted or more added according to taste. Chinese chili paste may be substituted (available in Chinese foodstores). Prawns may be shelled if desired.

☙ Shrimp with Mandarin Oranges

炒蝦仁

COLOR: PAGE 83

¾ lb. shrimp, shelled and deveined
1 tsp. cornstarch mixed with 2 tsps. dry sherry
4 Tbsps. oil
½ cup canned mandarin orange segments, drained
½ tsp. salt
½ tsp. sugar

Mix shrimp with cornstarch-sherry mixture. Let stand 3 minutes. Heat oil, and stir-fry shrimp just until color changes. Add mandarin orange segments, salt, and sugar, and stir-fry 30 seconds. Serve hot. Serves 3 as a main course. Serves 4–5 Chinese style.

🦐 Prawn Sesame Puffs   炸芝蔴蝦

COLOR: PAGE 93

4 prawns, shelled, slit deeply down back, deveined, and opened flat
½ tsp. salt
1 tsp. dry sherry
1 Tbsp. cornstarch
BATTER
    ½ cup all-purpose flour
    ½ tsp. baking powder
    ½ Tbsp. (black) sesame seeds
    ½ cup water

Sprinkle prawns with salt and sherry and let stand 10 minutes. Mix BATTER ingredients until smooth. Heat oil to hot (360°). Dip prawns first in cornstarch (shake off excess cornstarch) then in batter. Deep fry until just light brown. Drain. Cut each puff in three and serve hot with catsup as dip. Serves 2 as a main course. Serves 4–5 Chinese style or as an hors d'oeuvre.

🦐 Curried Cuttlefish   咖利魷魚

COLOR: PAGE 96

3 medium cuttlefish, cut open, cleaned, head, legs, and thin skin removed, scored in crisscross pattern on outside surface, and cut into 1-in. squares
SEASONINGS
    1 Tbsp. dry sherry
    1 tsp. ginger juice
    1 tsp. cornstarch
3 Tbsps. oil
½ cup pine nuts
½ cucumber, skinned, seeded, and cut into 1-in. cubes
1 tsp. salt
1 Tbsp. curry powder

Mix cuttlefish and SEASONINGS and let stand 2–3 minutes. Heat oil and stir-fry cuttlefish until firm and milky white (about 3–4 minutes). Add pine nuts, cucumber, salt, and curry powder. Stir briefly, until well blended. Serve hot. Serves 3–4 as a main course. Serves 6–7 Chinese style.

🦐 Crab with Green Peas   蟹肉青豆

COLOR: PAGE 90

1 can crabmeat, cartilage removed and broken into
   shreds
1 cup frozen green peas
SEASONINGS
   1 Tbsp. dry sherry
   $\frac{1}{3}$ cup chicken stock
   $\frac{1}{4}$ tsp. salt
   2–3 drops sesame oil
1 tsp. cornstarch mixed with 2 tsps. water

Heat oil and stir-fry crabmeat until coated with oil.
Add peas and SEASONINGS and stir-fry 1–1$\frac{1}{2}$ minutes.
Add cornstarch mixture and stir until thickened.
Serve hot. Serves 2 as a vegetable course. Serves 4
Chinese style.

🦐 Beancurd with Oysters   炒豆付蜊蝗

COLOR: PAGE 92

4 Tbsps. oil
1 leek, chopped finely
3 slices ginger
$\frac{1}{2}$ lb. oysters, washed
2 loaves beancurd, cut into 1$\frac{1}{2}$-in. cubes
SEASONINGS
   2 Tbsps. soy sauce
   2 Tbsps. dry sherry
   4 tsps. sugar
   $\frac{1}{2}$ tsp. chili sauce or powder (optional)
1 spring parsley, chopped finely

Heat oil and stir-fry leek and ginger 2–3 seconds. Add
oysters, beancurd, and SEASONINGS. Reduce heat to
medium and simmer 5 minutes. Remove to serving
dish, sprinkle with parsley, and serve hot. Serves 2
as a main course. Serves 4 Chinese style.

Serenity Pork (p. 126)

Coin Purse Eggs (p. 107); Spring Rolls for Summer (p. 112)

Shrimp with Mandarin Oranges (p. 77); Gold-Silver Chickens (p. 118)

83

Papaya and Celery Salad (p. 56); Seacliff Prawns (p. 77); Beef Sashlik (p. 133)

Salmon with Soybeans (p. 70); Meatballs with Grapes (p. 127); Spring Onion and Bean Sprout Soup (p. 140)

Veal with Lotus Root and Peas (p. 134); Three Sisters (p. 64); Mango and Cabbage
Salad (p. 56)

Pavilion Eggs (p. 108); Fish with Pine Nuts (p. 71); Cabbage with Apricots (p. 65)

Sauerkraut with Beef (p. 64); Phoenix Nest (p. 65); Pork Roulade (p. 128)

Coral and Pearls (p. 143); Autumn Treasure (p. 143)

Crab with Green Peas (p. 79); Spicy Pork Chops (p. 129); Spring Dream (p. 52)

7-11. Cloud Scroll Rolls (p. 105). 8. 9.

10. 11.

12-14. Small, filled omelets (Omelets with Spinach, p. 106).

13.

14.

15-22. Flower Buns (p. 110).

16.

17.

18.

19.

20.

21.

22.

23-27. Spring Rolls (p. 112).   24.

25.   26.   27.

28-30. Sunflower Meat Pies (p. 130).   29.   30.

31. Spring Dream (p. 52).

103

Eggs, Rolls, and Others

🍂 Egg Rolls

蛋 卷

COLOR: PAGE 24

$\frac{1}{4}$ lb. lean pork, shred-cut
$1\frac{1}{2}$ tsps. soy sauce
1 tsp. dry sherry
1 tsp. cornstarch
3 Tbsps. oil
1 cup shred-cut bamboo shoots
$\frac{1}{2}$ cup shred-cut Chinese mushrooms that have been soaked in lukewarm water until tender and stemmed
2 tsps. soy sauce
1 tsp. sugar
WRAPPINGS
    4 Tbsps. flour
    4 Tbsps. water
    4 eggs, beaten lightly
    $\frac{1}{2}$ Tbsp. salt
3 Tbsps. flour mixed with 3 Tbsps. water
oil for deep frying

Mix pork with soy sauce, sherry, and cornstarch. Heat oil and stir-fry pork until color changes. Add bamboo shoots and mushrooms, and stir-fry 2 minutes, then add soy sauce and sugar and stir well 2–3 times. Remove from heat and cool. Divide this meat mixture into 5 portions and set aside.

Add water to flour, mix well, add egg and salt, and beat well. Heat frying pan, thinly coat pan with

oil, and pour in ⅕ of egg batter to cover pan bottom. Fry over low heat until set. Remove from heat to cool slightly, peel egg sheet from pan with fingers, and set aside. Repeat process for 4 remaining egg sheets. Place ⅕ of meat mixture on each egg sheet, fold in both sides, and roll (see process photos, p. 102). Seal with flour and water mixture. Heat oil to medium (340°) and deep fry each roll until golden brown. Remove from oil and drain. Cut diagonally into 1-in. lengths and serve hot. Serves 2–3 as a main course. Serves 4–6 Chinese style or as an hors d'oeuvre.

🐚 Cloud Scroll Rolls   蒸如意蛋卷

COLOR: PAGE 25

3 eggs, beaten with 1 tsp. cornstarch and ½ tsp. salt
3 Tbsps. oil
¾ lb. ground pork
1 egg
1 tsp. cornstarch
SEASONINGS
    1 tsp. salt
    1 tsp. sugar
    1 Tbsp. dry sherry
    1 tsp. ginger juice
    1 Tbsp. finely chopped leek
½ small carrot, cut into 4-in. slivers (see process photos, p. 99)
3–4 stalks spinach, leaves separated, parboiled, and drained
1 Tbsp. flour mixed with 2 Tbsps. water

Heat 6-in. frying pan over low heat, thinly coat bottom of pan with oil, and pour in ¼ of egg mixture. Tip pan to spread egg mixture over pan bottom and fry until set. Remove from heat, cool slightly, and peel egg sheet from pan with fingers. Repeat process for 3 remaining egg sheets. Set aside. Heat 3 Tbsps. oil and stir-fry ½ of ground pork until color changes. Remove from heat and cool. Mix cooked pork with remaining ground pork, egg, cornstarch, and SEASONINGS. Divide this meat mixture into 4 portions. Place one egg sheet on a board, sprinkle lightly with cornstarch on one side and evenly spread with one portion of meat mixture (see process photos, p. 99). Place carrot slivers in a line on one side and spinach on the other side, and roll in from both sides. At the center where the rolls meet, apply the flour and water mixture as an adhesive. Repeat process with remaining egg sheets and meat mixture. Tightly wrap each roll with damp cloth, place in a preheated steamer, and steam over high heat 20 minutes. Remove from heat, remove cloth, and cool. Cut into ½-in. lengths. Serves 10 Chinese style or as an hors d'oeuvre.

❦ Omelets with Spinach 蛋餃菠菜

COLOR: PAGE 27

FILLING

- ½ ground pork
- 2 Tbsps. finely chopped onion
- ½ tsp. salt
- I tsp. soy sauce

3 eggs
I egg yolk
pinch salt
oil
I cup chicken stock or water
I Tbsp. soy sauce
2 tsps. cornstarch mixed with 2 Tbsps. water
3 Tbsps. oil
½ tsp. salt
½ lb. spinach, hard stems removed and halved

Mix all the ingredients for FILLING. Beat eggs with pinch salt (the extra egg yolk allows a brighter color). Heat a little oil in iron ladle, pour about I Tbsp. egg mixture into it, and spread evenly on the bottom to make a thin pancake, tipping ladle (see process photos, p. 100). When it starts to firm, place I tsp. filling in the center and fold in half to make a small omelet. Remove from ladle. Repeat process until filling and egg mixture are used up. Put omelets in pan, add stock and soy sauce, and simmer over low heat 10 minutes. Add cornstarch mixture and stir until thick-

ened. Set aside. Heat 3 Tbsps. oil, add ½ tsp. salt and stir-fry spinach 30 seconds. Place spinach on serving plate, arrange omelets on it, and pour over thickened broth. Serve hot. Serves 2–3 as a main course. Serves 6–8 Chinese style.

❦ Swatonese Egg Fu Yung 潮州芙蓉蛋

COLOR: PAGE 36

2 Tbsps. oil
½ cup roughly chopped salt-preserved turnips (see recipe, p. 55)
6 eggs, beaten lightly with pinch salt and dash white pepper

Heat oil in frying pan, stir-fry turnips 3–4 seconds, and spread evenly on pan. Add egg mixture and spread evenly by tipping pan. Cover and cook over low heat until set (about 5 minutes). Turn over carefully, taking care not to break shape, and cook another 2 minutes or until dried. Remove to serving plate and cut into wedges. Serve hot. Serves 2 as an egg course. Serves 5–6 Chinese style.

🦋 Vermicelli with Eggs   粉絲炒蛋

¼ lb. lean pork, shred-cut

MARINADE

    1 tsp. dry sherry

    1 tsp. soy sauce

    ¼ tsp. sugar

    2 tsps. water

2 Tbsps. oil

4 large dried Chinese mushrooms, soaked in luke-warm water until tender, stemmed, and shred-cut

4 spring onions, chopped

2 oz. transparent vermicelli, soaked in lukewarm water until tender and cut into 4-in. lengths

4 Tbsps. oil

½ tsp. salt

¼ cup soup stock

3 eggs, beaten with pinch salt

Mix MARINADE and marinate pork 5 minutes. Heat oil, stir-fry pork 3 minutes, add mushroom and spring onion, and stir-fry another 2 minutes. Set aside. Heat 4 Tbsps. oil, stir-fry vermicelli over medium-high heat, taking care it does not stick to pan. Sprinkle with salt and add soup stock very slowly, stirring and separating vermicelli. Add pork mixture and stir well. Trail in egg mixture and stir-fry 2 minutes. Serve hot. Serves 4 as an egg course. Serves 5–6 Chinese style.

🦋 Coin Purse Eggs   澆汁蛋

COLOR: PAGE 82

6 eggs

3 Tbsps. oil

1 cup small shrimp, shelled

¾ cup dried Chinese mushrooms, soaked in luke-warm water until tender, stemmed, and quartered

¾ cup canned bamboo shoots, cut into 1-in. pieces

SEASONINGS

    1 Tbsp. dry sherry

    dash pepper

    ½ tsp. salt

    2 Tbsps. soy sauce

2 tsps. cornstarch mixed with 1½ cups chicken stock or water

Cook each egg individually in an oiled ladle or in basting cups. Remove to serving plate. Heat 3 Tbsps. oil, stir-fry shrimp until color changes, and add mushroom and bamboo shoot. Stir-fry 30 seconds. Add SEASONINGS and thicken with cornstarch mixture. Pour over eggs. Serve hot. Serves 3 as a main course. Serves 5–6 Chinese style.

Note: One-half cup canned champignons may be substituted for Chinese mushrooms.

❧ Pavilion Eggs

黃 寶 塔

COLOR: PAGE 87

2 eggs
¼ tsp. salt
1½ cups all-purpose flour, sifted
1½ cups water
2 Tbsps. finely chopped leek
oil
4 eggs
2 tsps. soy sauce or ¼ tsp. salt
dash pepper
3 Tbsps. oil

Beat 2 eggs, then add salt, flour and water alternately, a little at a time, beating constantly to form a smooth batter. Mix in chopped leek. Heat 9-inch frying pan over medium heat and brush lightly with oil. Pour in 5–6 Tbsps. batter and tip pan so batter covers pan bottom evenly. Fry until just slightly brown, then reverse and brown other side. Repeat process until batter used. Makes 6 pancakes. Set aside. Beat 4 eggs with soy sauce or salt and pepper. Heat pan, add oil, pour in egg mixture, and scramble. Fold each pancake in quarters, lift one fold, insert scrambled eggs, and fold back pancake (see color photograph). Serve hot. Serves 4 as a main course. Serves 8–10 Chinese style.

❧ Piney Cliff Eggs

松崖芙蓉

COLOR: PAGE 93

3 eggs, beaten with pinch salt
2 Tbsps. oil
¼ lb. pork, cut into bite-sized slices
SEASONINGS
    2 tsps. soy sauce
    1 tsp. dry sherry
    1 tsp. cornstarch
3 Tbsps. oil
4–5 stalks spinach, hard stems removed and cut into 3-in. lengths
1 Tbsp. minced leek
2 tsps. dry sherry
½ tsp. salt

Heat 2 Tbsps. oil and scramble eggs until just firm. Cut into chunks with spatula and set aside. Mix pork with SEASONINGS, heat 3 Tbsps. oil, and stir-fry pork until color changes. Add spinach, scrambled egg, leek, sherry, and salt, and stir-fry 30 seconds. Serve hot. Serves 2 as an egg course. Serves 4 Chinese style.

Apology: I forgot to add the pork when the photo was taken, but thought it best to keep it in the recipe anyway, even if you can't see it in the photo, and add this apology in the hope this oversight will be forgiven when you enjoy this dish.

🦪 Blossoms on Snow   雪 中 花

COLOR: PAGE 94

4 eggs
½ tsp. salt
2 cups chicken stock
½ leek, chopped finely
1 slice boiled ham, chopped finely
3 sprigs parsley, chopped finely
1 Tbsp. sesame oil

Beat eggs with salt, stock, and leek. Pour mixture into heat-resistant dessert dishes and steam over low heat for 15 minutes. Mix ham, parsley, and sesame oil and sprinkle over firm custard. Serve hot or at room temperature. Serves 2 as an egg course. Serves 4–5 Chinese style.

Note: A large container or small, individual serving dishes may be used to steam the custard.

🦪 Chinese Omelet   大 蛋 餃

COLOR: PAGE 95

¼ lb. shrimp, shelled and deveined
SEASONINGS
    1 tsp. cornstarch
    1 tsp. ginger juice
    1 tsp. dry sherry
3 Tbsps. oil
4 eggs, beaten with 1 tsp. salt
3 Tbsps. oil
2 dried Chinese mushrooms, soaked in lukewarm water until tender, stemmed, and diced
2 Tbsps. green peas
½ cup water

Mix shrimp and SEASONINGS and let stand 2–3 minutes. Heat 3 Tbsps. oil and stir-fry shrimp until color changes. Set aside. Heat 3 Tbsps. oil over medium heat, add egg, and cook until firm. Do not scramble. Add shrimp, mushroom, and peas. Pour water down sides of pan, cover pan, and simmer 1 minute. Serve hot. Serves 2 as an egg course. Serves 4–6 Chinese style.

🍂 Flower Buns   蒸花卷

COLOR: PAGE 27

3–5 tsps. dry yeast
1½ cups warm water
1½ Tbsps. sugar
5 cups flour
½ Tbsp. salt
2 tsps. baking powder
sesame oil
salt
5 Tbsps. finely chopped ham

Dissolve yeast in warm water with sugar. Sift flour with salt. When yeast begins to bubble, add to sifted flour, mix until firm, and knead on lightly floured board until dough is smooth. Place dough in bowl, cover with damp cloth, and let stand 3 hours in a warm place. When dough has risen, knead again with baking powder. Replace in bowl, cover with damp cloth, and let rise 30 minutes. Knead again about 20 times. Divide dough into 4 portions. With a rolling pin, roll out each portion into ⅛-inch-thick round. Brush each round with sesame oil and sprinkle with salt and ¼ of chopped ham. Roll like a jelly roll; the roll should be about 2 inches in diameter.

Cut roll into 3-inch lengths. Cut through ⅔ length of center axis of each 3-inch piece (see process photos, pages 100–101), forming a short trunk with two "legs." Twist "legs" 90° so that cut layers of ham-filled roll face upward. Then, holding piece by both ends, in one swift motion stretch dough while twisting 180° (or more) and curling so that the two ends meet. Pinch ends together and place on damp cloth in a steamer with pinched ends down. Steam over high heat 15 minutes. Serve hot. Makes about 12 buns.

Note: Buns may be reheated in steamer.

🍂 Sizzling Rice   什錦蓋飯

COLOR: PAGE 29

1½ cups moist-cooked rice
3 Tbsps. oil
½ lb. shrimp, shelled and deveined
½ cup canned champignons, halved
½ cut canned bamboo shoots, sliced
2 Tbsps. frozen green peas
SEASONINGS
    1 Tbsp. soy sauce
    1 tsp. ginger juice
    1 Tbsp. vinegar
    1 Tbsp. dry sherry
    1 Tbsp. sugar
    1 tsp. salt

2½ cups chicken stock
2½ Tbsps. cornstarch mixed with 4 Tbsps. water
oil for deep frying

Spread an even, thin layer of cooked rice on cookie sheet or on the inside of roasting pan, pressing firmly to make the layer uniform. Dry rice in the sun or in a very slow oven until hard and brittle. Break into 3-inch pieces. Start heating oil for deep frying to hot (360°). At the same time, heat 3 Tbsps. oil in a frying pan, add shrimp, and stir-fry until color changes. Add champignons, bamboo shoots, peas, SEASONINGS, and stock and stir until liquid boils. Add cornstarch mixture and stir until thickened. Remove to bowl. Place dried rice pieces in hot oil and deep fry until crispy (about 1 minute). Do not brown. Drain. Place crispy rice on serving plate while hot and serve with separate bowl of shrimp mixture immediately. At the table, pour mixture over hot rice. The resulting sizzling, crackling "music" gives this dish its name and is one of its great attractions. Serves 3 as a main course. Serves 6–7 Chinese style.

🍎 Chilled Noodles with Spicy Sauce 冷拌麵

COLOR: PAGE 28

6 oz. chicken, white or dark meat, as preferred
½ cup shred-cut cucumber
½ cup shred-cut ham
SAUCE
    1 cup chicken stock
    4 Tbsps. soy sauce
    2 Tbsps. vinegar
    ½ tsp. sugar
    1 Tbsp. chili oil (or Tabasco sauce)
    4 Tbsps. finely chopped leek or onion
10 oz. dried Chinese noodles
2 Tbsps. sesame oil

Put chicken in boiling water and cook until tender (about 25 minutes). Remove from water and cool, then bone and shred-cut. Mix SAUCE ingredients and set aside. Bring ample water to boil and add noodles. When the water boils, pour in 1 cup cold water and bring to boil again. Remove from heat and drain noodles, then spread noodles on a large plate, sprinkle with sesame oil, and fan until cool. Arrange on serving plate with chicken, cucumber, and ham on the top, and serve with sauce. Serves 1.

Note: If noodles are rinsed in cold water after boiling, flavor will be reduced. Cooked chicken may be used.

111

❀ Spring Rolls for Summer　炸春卷

COLOR: PAGE 82

FILLING

    3 Tbsps. oil
    ½ lb. lean pork, shred-cut
    3 Tbsps. oil
    2 cups shred-cut cabbage
    2 cups shred-cut green pepper
    ½ cup shred-cut Chinese mushrooms that have
        been soaked in lukewarm water until tender
        and stemmed
    1 Tbsp. soy sauce
    ½ tsp. salt
    1 Tbsp. cornstarch mixed with 3 Tbsps. water

WRAPPINGS

    2 cups all-purpose flour
    2 cups water
2 tsps. cornstarch mixed with 1 Tbsp. water
oil for deep frying
lettuce

Heat 3 Tbsps. oil and stir-fry pork until color changes. Remove to bowl. Heat 3 Tbsps. oil and stir-fry cabbage, green pepper, and mushroom for 2 minutes. Add pork, soy sauce, and salt and stir 2–3 times. Add cornstarch mixture and stir until thickened. Cool.
WRAPPINGS: Heat a 6- or 9-inch nonstick frypan over medium-high heat. Using a pastry brush, quickly and uniformly brush a 6-inch round of batter on the hot pan. As it begins to dry, brush on more batter. Two or three brushings will produce a very thin, translucent wrapping. When the edges crinkle and pull away from the pan, the wrapping can be pulled away in one quick motion. This a very simple process, but may need a little experimentation with thickness of batter, heat, and amount of batter in the brush before you discover the formula best for you. The finished wrapping should be white, translucent, and have thin, crinkly edges. If a nonstick pan is not used, a small amount of oil should be spread on the pan surface with kitchen paper for each wrapping.

Place 1½ Tbsps. filling on the lower half of each wrapping. Fold bottom edge up, roll to cover filling, tuck ends in and complete rolling (see process photos, p. 102). Seal edges with cornstarch and water mixture. Heat oil to hot (360°) and deep fry until golden brown. Roll in lettuce. Serve hot or at room temperature. Makes 20 rolls.

🍎 Kublai Khan Macaroni 元朝通心麵

COLOR: PAGE 96

6 oz. macaroni
3 Tbsps. oil
1 lb. ground pork
1 cup canned sliced champignons
1 clove garlic, minced
SEASONINGS
    1 Tbsp. soy sauce
    4 Tbsps. bean paste
    2 Tbsps. sugar
    1 cup chicken stock
    2–3 drops sesame oil
1 Tbsp. cornstarch mixed with 3 Tbsps. water

Boil macaroni as directed on package, drain, and remove to serving plate. Heat 3 Tbsps. oil, add pork, champignons, and garlic, and stir-fry until pork changes color. Reduce heat to medium, add SEASONINGS, and bring to boil. Add cornstarch mixture and stir until thickened. Pour over macaroni and serve hot. Serves 4–5 as a main course. Serves 10–12 Chinese style.

Poultry

🍎 Fried Chicken with Peking Sauce

油淋鷄

COLOR: PAGE 22

SAUCE

    3 Tbsps. chopped leek
    1 tsp. chopped ginger
    $\frac{1}{2}$ tsp. finely chopped garlic
    3 Tbsps. soy sauce
    1 tsp. sugar
    2 Tbsps. vinegar
    1 Tbsp. sesame oil

1 fryer chicken

MARINADE

    $1\frac{1}{2}$ tsps. salt
    2 Tbsps. soy sauce
    3 Tbsps. dry sherry
    dash pepper

2 Tbsps. soy sauce

oil for deep frying

Mix SAUCE ingredients and set aside. Clean chicken, cut in half down breastbone. Rub chicken with MARINADE and marinate 15–20 minutes. Rub chicken with soy sauce again. Heat oil to medium (340°) and deep fry chicken until done (about 15 minutes). Remove from oil, drain, and separate legs and wings and cut crosswise (with bone). Arrange on serving plate and pour sauce over chicken just before serving. Serve hot or at room temperature. Serves 2–3 as a main course. Serves 5–6 Chinese style.

☙ Chicken and Chrysanthemums   炒菊花鷄絲

COLOR: PAGE 23

1 lb. chicken fillet, shred-cut
1 Tbsp. dry sherry
1 egg white
3 Tbsps. oil
1 Tbsp. oil
2 chrysanthemum flowers, washed with salted water, petals separated, and drained
1 tsp. salt
dash pepper
pinch sugar

Mix chicken with sherry and egg white. Heat 3 Tbsps. oil, stir-fry chicken until color changes, and set aside. Heat 1 Tbsp. oil, stir-fry chrysanthemum petals 15 seconds, add chicken, and stir 2–3 times. Season with salt, pepper, and sugar. Serve hot. Serves 2 as a main course. Serves 4 Chinese style

☙ Chicken and Vegetables with Chili   炒辣子鷄絲

COLOR: PAGE 29

2 Tbsps. oil
1 small carrot, shred-cut
1 stalk celery, shred-cut
2 cups shred-cut green pepper
3 Tbsps. oil
½ lb. chicken meat, shred-cut
2 red chili peppers, seeded and chopped roughly (or 1 tsp. Tabasco sauce)
1 tsp. salt
½ tsp. sugar

Heat 2 Tbsps. oil and stir-fry carrot 30 seconds, then add celery and green pepper and stir 3–4 times. Remove. Heat 3 Tbsps. oil and stir-fry chicken until color changes. Add vegetables and red chili pepper, salt, and sugar. Stir 2–3 times. Serve hot. Serves 2 as a main course. Serves 4–5 Chinese style.

❦ White Jade 白 玉

½ lb. ground chicken filet (put through grinder 2–3 times)
1 egg white
½ tsp. salt
2 Tbsps. dry sherry
½ cup canned and drained (or dried, cooked) bird's nest
green peas or carrot shreds

Combine chicken, egg white, salt, and sherry and mix well. In a lightly oiled Chinese porcelain soupspoon (or oiled small foil baking cups), place a layer of chicken mixture one-third the height of the container, add a layer of bird's nest, then chicken mixture in equal amounts. Place filled spoons (or foil cups) in a preheated steamer and steam 15 or 20 minutes. Garnish decoratively with peas, carrot shreds, or as desired. Serves 3 as a main course. Serves 6 Chinese style.

Note: Any container, large or small, may be used for this layered dish. If a large container is used, the firm mixture may be cut in diamond or other decorative shapes.

❦ Elegant Chicken 蒸子鷄

COLOR: PAGE 31

1 3-lb. fryer chicken
3 Tbsps. dry sherry
1 Tbsps. ginger juice
3 Tbsps. salt mixed with 2 Tbsps. freshly ground pepper
2 spring onions, halved
oil for deep frying
LEMON DIP
    1 cup chicken broth from steamed chicken
    juice of one lemon
    ¼ tsp. salt

Wash chicken and pat dry. Rub cavity and skin of chicken with sherry, ginger juice, and salt-pepper mixture. Place spring onion in cavity and let stand 2 hours. Place chicken in deep dish and steam until tender (about 35 minutes). Discard onion. Drain chicken and pat dry, reserving 1 cup liquid for lemon dip. Heat oil to medium (340°) and deep fry steamed whole chicken until golden brown. Drain on absorbent paper. Cut chicken into bite-sized pieces and serve hot with lemon dip.

LEMON DIP: Mix ingredients and pour in small serving dish.

Serves 3–4 as a main course. Serves 6–8 Chinese style.

🦃 Swatonese Chicken Sauté   潮州鷄

COLOR: PAGE 34

MARINADE
  2 tsps. dry sherry
  2 tsps. ginger juice
  2 Tbsps. soy sauce
  2 tsps. cornstarch
  dash white pepper
1 lb. chicken filet, cut diagonally into $\frac{1}{4}$-in.-thick
  bite-sized slices
2 Tbsps. oil
2 Tbsps. anise pepper (whole), crushed lightly (or 1
  tsp. ground black pepper)
4 Tbsps. water
2 Tbsps. oil
pinch salt
4 cups spinach or chard that has been cut into 2-in.
  pieces

Mix MARINADE and marinate chicken 10 minutes.
Heat oil and stir-fry anise pepper over low heat 3
minutes. Discard pepper. Add chicken and water and
stir-fry 3 minutes. Remove to serving plate. Heat oil,
add pinch salt, stir-fry greens 30 seconds, and arrange
around chicken. Serve hot. Serves 2 as a main course.
Serves 4–5 Chinese style.

Note: Chicken cut diagonally should curl when stir-
fried.

🦃 Chicken with Black Bean Sauce   豆豉鷄

1 fryer chicken, cut into $1\frac{1}{2}$-in. pieces (with bone)
MARINADE
  2 Tbsps. dry sherry
  1 tsp. ginger juice
  2 tsps. soy sauce
  1 tsp. cornstarch
4 Tbsps. oil
4 Tbsps. fermented black beans, coarsely chopped
$\frac{1}{4}$ cup water
2 small cucumbers, sliced thinly

Mix MARINADE and marinate chicken 10 minutes.
Heat oil and stir-fry black beans a few seconds. Add
chicken and stir well over high heat until color
changes. Add water, cover, and continue cooking 10
minutes. Remove to serving plate, garnish with cucumber slices, and serve hot. Serves 3–4 as a main
course. Serves 6–8 Chinese style.

Gold-Silver Chickens 金銀鷄

COLOR: PAGE 83

GOLD
1 fryer chicken
1 tsp. freshly ground black pepper
1 tsp. salt
3 Tbsps. dry sherry
1 leek, cut diagonally into 2-in. lengths
4 slices ginger
SEASONINGS
    5 Tbsps. soy sauce
    3 Tbsps. sesame oil
    1 Tbsp. sugar
    1 Tbsp. dry sherry
    1 cup liquid obtained from steaming chicken

Rub chicken with pepper and salt, then sprinkle with sherry. Insert leek and ginger in cavity and let stand 15–20 minutes. Place chicken in bowl and steam until tender (about 30 minutes). Discard ginger and leek. Heat SEASONINGS in frying pan, place chicken in liquid over low heat, and baste chicken until evenly brown.

SILVER
1 fryer chicken
$1\frac{1}{2}$ tsps. salt
1 stalk leek, cut diagonally into 2-in. lengths
4 slices ginger
$\frac{3}{4}$ cup dry sherry

Rub chicken with salt, insert leek and ginger in cavity, place in bowl and let stand 5–10 minutes. Pour sherry over chicken, turn two or three times, and let chicken stand in sherry 2–3 hours. Steam chicken until tender (about 30 minutes). Discard ginger and leek.

Arrange the chickens together in one serving plate, and serve at room temperature. Serves 6–8 as a main course. Serves 10–12 Chinese style.

Stewed Garlic Chicken 紅燒鷄

1 fryer chicken, cut into 2-in. pieces with bone
1 Tbsp. soy sauce
1 Tbsp. oil
2 cloves garlic
1 Tbsp. dry sherry
2 small onions, quartered
4 cups chicken stock (or water)
2 Tbsps. bean paste
$\frac{1}{2}$ tsp. salt
1 tsp. sugar

Sprinkle chicken with soy sauce and let stand 10 minutes. Heat oil, stir-fry garlic 2–3 seconds, add chicken and sherry, and stir 3–4 times. Add onion and stir-fry until coated with oil. Add remaining ingredients, lower heat to medium, cover, and simmer until tender (15–20 minutes). Serve hot. Serves 2–3 as a main course. Serves 5–6 Chinese style.

❦ Chicken with Lemon Sauce 檸檬汁鷄

COLOR: PAGE 91

1 lb. chicken filet, cut into bite-sized pieces

SEASONINGS A

    1 Tbsp. dry sherry
    1 Tbsp. soy sauce
    $\frac{1}{2}$ egg white
    1 Tbsp. cornstarch

3 Tbsps. oil

SEASONINGS B

    juice of $\frac{1}{2}$ lemon
    $\frac{1}{2}$ Tbsp. catsup
    $\frac{1}{2}$ cup chicken stock
    $1\frac{1}{2}$ Tbsps. sugar
    $\frac{1}{2}$ tsp. salt

1 Tbsp. cornstarch mixed with 2 Tbsps. water
$\frac{1}{2}$ lemon, sliced, and slices halved

Mix chicken with SEASONINGS A. Heat oil and stir-fry chicken until color changes. Add SEASONINGS B and stir-fry 3–4 minutes. Add cornstarch mixture and stir until thickened. Garnish with lemon slices. Serve hot. Serves 2 as a main course. Serves 4 Chinese style.

❦ Hawaiian-Chinese (and vice versa) Chicken 夏威夷炸鷄

COLOR: PAGE 94

1 fryer chicken, cut into 2-in. pieces with bone
1 tsp. salt
2 Tbsps. dry sherry
oil for deep frying
2 Tbsps. oil
$\frac{1}{2}$ lb. spinach, hard stems removed
$\frac{1}{2}$ tsp. salt
1 cup liquid from canned pineapple
2 cups chicken stock
$\frac{1}{2}$ tsp. salt
1 Tbsp. soy sauce
1 tsp. cornstarch mixed with 2 Tbsps. water
4 canned pineapple rings, halved

Mix chicken with salt and sherry and let stand 10 minutes. Heat oil to hot (360°) and deep fry chicken until golden brown. Drain. Heat 2 Tbsps. oil, add spinach and $\frac{1}{2}$ tsp. salt, and stir-fry until just coated with oil. Bring stock and pineapple liquid to boil, add $\frac{1}{2}$ tsp. salt, soy sauce, and cornstarch mixture, and stir until thickened. Add chicken and spinach to liquid, stir 1–2 times, and remove to serving dish. Garnish with pineapple. Serve hot. Serves 2–3 as a main course. Serves 4–6 Chinese style.

Swatonese Braised Goose 潮州紅燒鵝

COLOR: PAGE 32

1 4½–5 lb. lean, tender goose (or duck)
3 Tbsps. salt
2 tsps. white pepper
3 stalks spring onion, halved
3 Tbsps. oil

SEASONINGS

    10 cloves star anise
    3⅓ Tbsps. whole anise pepper (or 2 Tbsps. black
       peppercorns)
    2 sticks cinnamon
    4 Tbsps. brown sugar
2 1-in. cubes ginger, crushed
1½ cups soy sauce
1 Tbsp. salt
4 cups water

SAUCE

    4 cloves garlic, chopped finely
    ¾ cup water
    1 tsp. vinegar
    2 tsps. sugar dissolved in 2 Tbsps. hot water

Wash goose and pat dry with kitchen paper. Rub cavity and skin with salt and pepper. Insert spring onion in cavity and let stand 3 hours. In a large pot or Dutch oven, heat oil over low heat, add star anise, pepper, cinnamon, and sugar (in this order), stir about 3 minutes, then add ginger, soy sauce, and salt, and increase heat to high. When liquid boils, add 1 cup water and bring to boil again. Add goose and cook, basting and turning, until skin is golden brown (about 10 minutes). Add remaining water, bring to boil, then cover and simmer over medium heat 2½ hours, turning and basting every 15 minutes. Keep liquid always the same level by adding water every half hour. Remove and cool on rack. Discard spices and reserve liquid in bowl

SAUCE: Mix all ingredients and place in sauce dish.

SERVING: Separate drumsticks and breast from goose; debone and slice thinly at an angle. Halve the remaining goose, chop crosswise into bite-sized pieces (with bone), and place on serving plate. Arrange sliced meat on top of chopped meat, and moisten meat with 5–6 Tbsps. gravy. Serve with sauce and gravy as dips. For hors d'oeuvres, serve only sliced breast meat. Serves 5 as a main course. Serves 7–10 Chinese style.

🍎 Szechwan Smoked Duck   樟茶鴨

COLOR: PAGE 24

1 duck, cleaned
2 Tbsps. salt, mixed with 1 tsp. potassium nitrate
   (saltpetre)

SEASONINGS
   3 Tbsps. salt
   1 clove star anise
   1 Tbsp. whole anise pepper (or 1½ tsps. ground
      black pepper)
   1 leek, cut into 3-in. lengths
   5 slices ginger
   3 Tbsps. dried tangerine (or orange) peel
1 Tbsp. green tea leaves
oil for deep frying

Rub skin and cavity of duck with salt and potassium nitrate mixture and let stand 3 hours. Place SEASONINGS and ample water in saucepan, bring to boil, and cool. Soak duck in seasoned water 7 hours, occasionally turning. Drain and pat dry. Line bottom of large saucepan with foil and add tea leaves. Place a rack in the pan and place duck on it. Cover pan with foil, cover tightly with lid, and heat (medium heat) 15 minutes. Remove duck from pan, place in a preheated steamer, and steam 40–50 minutes. Pat thoroughly dry and hang in a well-ventilated place overnight. Before serving, heat oil to medium (340°) and deep fry until crisp. Remove and drain. Cut into bite-sized pieces and serve hot or at room temperature. Serves 4 as a main course. Serves 8–10 Chinese style.

Note: The secret of crisp-skinned fried duck is to have the skin completely dry before deep frying. A damp skin will not crisp. Hang the duck in a well-ventilated room overnight or in front of a fan for 4–5 hours to dry the skin thoroughly.

☙ Stuffed Duck 米塞鴨

COLOR: PAGE 25

1 duck, cleaned
1 cup rice, washed, soaked overnight, and drained
¼ cup diced dried Chinese mushrooms that have been soaked in lukewarm water until tender and stemmed
¼ cup diced boiled ham
¼ cup diced canned bamboo shoots or water chestnuts
2 Tbsps. green peas

SEASONINGS
    ½ tsp. salt
    2 Tbsps. soy sauce
    2 Tbsps. dry sherry

3 Tbsps. dry sherry
3 Tbsps. soy sauce
1 tsp. powdered anise pepper (or black pepper)
oil for deep frying

Parboil duck and drain. Place rice, mushroom, ham, bamboo shoots, green peas, and SEASONINGS with 1 cup water in pot, bring to boil, and cook over medium heat until liquid is absorbed. Remove and cool. Stuff cooked rice mixture in cavity of duck. Seal with toothpicks or sew with thread. Rub skin of duck with sherry, soy sauce, and powdered anise pepper. Put duck on plate, place in a preheated steamer, and steam until tender (about 1½ hours) or boil in about 4 cups water. Remove and pat completely dry. Heat oil to hot (360°) and deep fry duck until brown (or bake in hot oven). Remove to serving plate and decorate with preserved sugared ginger and parsley. Cut into 3 pieces (as pictured) or carve Western style and serve hot. Serves 3–4 as a main course. Serves 8–10 Chinese style.

Note: Thicken 1 cup gravy from the steamed duck with 2 tsps. cornstarch and pour over duck before serving, if desired. A crisp-skinned duck takes time to prepare (see *Note* to Szechwan Smoked Duck), but is worth the extra effort.

Pork, Mutton

❧ Braised Lamb with Garlic　紅燒羊肉

COLOR: PAGE 28

2 lbs. lamb (or mutton) shoulder chops
20 cloves garlic
1 leek, cut into 3-in. lengths
5 slices ginger
SEASONINGS
    2 cloves star anise
    1 Tbsp. whole anise pepper
    5 Tbsps. soy sauce
    2 Tbsps. dry sherry
oil for deep frying
2 tsps. cornstarch mixed with 1 Tbsp. water

Parboil lamb in ample water and discard water. Place lamb, garlic, leek, ginger, and SEASONINGS with water to cover in pot, cover, and bring to boil over high heat. Reduce heat to low and simmer until tender (about 1 hour). Remove lamb and drain, reserving liquid and garlic. Heat oil to medium and deep fry lamb until crisp (or bake in hot [425°] oven). Heat 1 cup liquid obtained from cooking lamb, add cornstarch mixture, and stir until thickened. Arrange lamb and garlic on serving plate and pour gravy over lamb. Serve hot or at room temperature. Serves 2 as a main course. Serves 4–6 Chinese style.

Note: When deep frying, cover pan to prevent oil from spattering.

🍎 Fried Pork

COLOR: PAGE 27

炸里脊

1 lb. lean, tender pork, cut into about 22 pieces
MARINADE
 2 Tbsps. dry sherry
 2 Tbsps. soy sauce
BATTER
 2 Tbsps. cornstarch
 4 Tbsps. flour
 2 Tbsps. finely chopped leek or onion
 1 egg white, beaten lightly
oil for deep frying
lettuce leaves
2 tsps. salt mixed with 2 tsps. freshly ground pepper

Mix pork with MARINADE and marinate 5 minutes. Add BATTER ingredients and mix well to coat each piece of pork. Heat oil to medium (340°), add 6 pieces of pork at one time, and deep fry until golden brown. Remove from oil and drain. Arrange on serving plate with lettuce leaves. Serve hot with salt-and-pepper mixture as dip. Serves 3–4 as a main course. Serves 6–7 Chinese style.

🍎 Piquant Pig's Feet

COLOR: PAGE 26

紅燒猪脚

6 pig's feet, cleaned and halved lengthwise
2 leeks, cut into 3-in. lengths
6 slices ginger
2 cloves star anise
1 Tbsp. whole anise pepper (or 2 tsps. black pepper-corns)
5 Tbsps. soy sauce
3 Tbsps. dry sherry
2 pieces red fermented beancurd

Place pig's feet in boiling water and boil over high heat 1 hour. Remove, wash with water, and drain. Bring an ample amount of water or stock to boil and add feet with all remaining ingredients. Cover, and simmer until feet are done (about 2 hours). Serve hot, at room temperature, or chilled. Serves 3–4 as an appetizer. Serves 6–8 Chinese style.

🍎 Boiled White Pork

白切肉

1 2-lb. pork roast
1-in. cube ginger, crushed
1 stalk leek, cut into 4-in. lengths
3 Tbsps. dry sherry

SAUCE

　　1 clove garlic, grated

　　4 Tbsps. soy sauce

Place pork with ginger, leek, sherry, and water to cover in large saucepan and bring to boil over high heat. Reduce heat to low, cover, and simmer until soft (1½ hours). Remove, place pork between two boards weighted with a large bowl or pot of water 20 minutes, and slice thinly. Mix SAUCE ingredients and serve as dip or poured over pork. Serve chilled. Serves 3–4 as a main course. Serves 8–10 Chinese style.

🐷 Stir-Fried Pork　　　炒蒜頭肉片

MARINADE

　　2 tsps. dry sherry

　　8 cloves garlic, grated

　　4 tsps. fish sauce (or 5 tsps. soy sauce)

　　1 tsp. soy sauce

　　½ tsp. sugar

　　½ tsp. cornstarch

1 lb. lean pork, cut into bite-sized slices (⅛-in. thick)

3 Tbsps. oil

6 cloves garlic, crushed

4 Tbsps. water

Mix MARINADE and marinate pork 10 minutes. Heat

oil, brown and discard crushed garlic. Stir-fry pork over high heat until color changes, add water, cover, and continue cooking 3 minutes. Serve hot. Serves 4 as a main course. Serves 5–6 Chinese style.

🐷 Garlic Pork with Eggplant　　肉燉茄子

3 Tbsps. oil

½ garlic bulb, cloves skinned and crushed

3 lbs. small eggplants, peeled lengthwise in ½-in. alternate stripes and cut into ½-in. slices

1 Tbsp. oil

1 bulb garlic, cloves skinned and crushed

1 lb. uncured bacon (pork flank), cut into 1 × 1 × 1½-in. chunks

1 Tbsp. soy sauce

1 cup water

2 Tbsps. small dried shrimp, soaked until just tender

Heat 3 Tbsps. oil, brown ½ bulb crushed garlic, and discard garlic. Add eggplant and stir-fry until coated with oil. Set aside. Heat 1 Tbsp. oil in Dutch oven, brown 1 bulb crushed garlic, add pork, and brown. Add soy sauce and water, cover, reduce heat to medium, and cook 30 minutes. Arrange shrimp on pork, top with eggplant, cover, reduce heat to medium-low, and cook until tender (about 20 minutes). Serve hot. Serves 4–5 as a main course. Serves 6–8 Chinese style.

🐷 Pork with Preserved Mustard Greens

炒蓋蘭肉片

COLOR: PAGE 37

1 lb. lean pork, cut into bite-sized slices ($\frac{1}{8}$-in. thick)

MARINADE

    1 Tbsp. dry sherry

    pinch salt

    $\frac{1}{2}$ tsp. cornstarch

2 Tbsps. oil

4 cups shred-cut (or cut into bite-sized lengths) preserved mustard greens (or $\frac{1}{2}$ cup canned preserved mustard greens, drained)

4 tsps. sugar

$\frac{1}{2}$ tsp. cornstarch mixed with 2 Tbsps. water

Mix pork with MARINADE and marinate 5 minutes. Heat oil and stir-fry pork until color changes. Add mustard greens and sugar, stir-fry 1 minute, add cornstarch mixture, and stir well until thickened. Serve hot. Serves 4 as a main course. Serves 6–7 Chinese style.

Note: Preserved Chinese mustard greens should be available in Chinese foodstores or restaurants.

🐷 Serenity Pork

東坡肉

COLOR: PAGE 81

1 lb. slab uncured bacon (pork flank)

SEASONINGS

    $\frac{1}{2}$ leek, cut into 2-in. lengths

    3 slices ginger

    1 Tbsp. dry sherry

1 Tbsp. oil

MARINADE

    $1\frac{1}{2}$ Tbsps. soy sauce

    1 clove star anise

    1 tsp. whole anise pepper (or $\frac{1}{2}$ tsp. ground black pepper)

    1 tsp. fresh orange peel

$\frac{1}{2}$ lb. spinach, hard stems removed and leaves halved

2 Tbsps. oil

$\frac{1}{2}$ tsp. salt

24 canned water chestnuts, loquats, or lychees

SAUCE

    $\frac{1}{2}$ cup juice from steamed pork

    2 Tbsps. cornstarch

Heat 1 Tbsp. oil in Dutch oven, add pork and SEASONINGS, and brown pork. Cover and simmer over low heat 15–20 minutes. Discard leek and ginger, place pork in bowl with MARINADE, marinate 15 minutes, then steam until soft (about 1 hour). Remove to serving plate (reserving liquid), cut pork slab in half crosswise. Heat 2 Tbsps. oil, add spinach and salt, and

stir-fry until just tender. Garnish pork with spinach and canned water chestnuts, loquats, or lychees. Heat ½ cup liquid from steamed pork in small saucepan, add cornstarch mixture, and stir until thickened. Pour sauce over pork. Serve hot. Serves 4–5 as a main course. Serves 10 Chinese style.

Note: This dish goes very well with mashed potatoes.

❁ Meatballs with Grapes 葡萄燴肉丸

COLOR: PAGE 85

MEATBALLS
- ½ lb. ground pork
- 3½ Tbsps. bread crumbs (or wheat germ)
- ½ leek, chopped finely
- 1 egg
- ½ tsp. salt
- ⅓ cup finely chopped canned water chestnuts (or bamboo shoots)

1 tsp. cornstarch mixed with 3 Tbsps. water
oil for deep frying
½ cup chicken stock
¼ lb. ham, cubed
1 cup canned green grapes (or fresh muscat grapes, peeled)

SEASONINGS
- 1 Tbsp. soy sauce
- 1 Tbsp. dry sherry
- ⅓ tsp. salt

2 tsps. cornstarch mixed with 2 Tbsps. water

Mix MEATBALL ingredients well and shape into walnut-sized meatballs (about 1 Tbsp. of mixture). Coat hands with cornstarch mixture and roll each meatball until just covered with cornstarch. Heat oil to hot (360°) and deep fry until golden brown. Drain. Heat stock, then add ham and grapes just before boiling starts. Add SEASONINGS and fried meatballs. Add cornstarch mixture and stir until thickened. Serve hot. Serves 3 as a main course. Serves 5–6 Chinese style.

🐖 Pork Roulade   猪 肉 卷

COLOR: PAGE 88

MARINADE

    1 tsp. soy sauce

    2 tsps. dry sherry

    1 clove garlic, sliced thinly or minced

    1 tsp. sesame oil

    dash cayenne pepper

1 lb. lean pork roast, cut into $\frac{1}{3} \times 4 \times 4$-in. slices

3 Tbsps. oil

1 cup canned bamboo shoots, shred-cut

8 medium dried Chinese mushrooms, soaked in luke-
    warm water until tender, stemmed, and shred-cut

SEASONINGS

    2 tsps. soy sauce

    1 Tbsp. dry sherry

    $\frac{1}{2}$ tsp. salt

Mix MARINADE and marinate pork 10 minutes. Heat oil, add bamboo shoot and mushroom, stir-fry until coated with oil, add SEASONINGS, and stir-fry 30 seconds. Place ample portion of bamboo shoot and mushroom on each pork slice, roll tightly, and secure with toothpick. Bake in preheated medium oven (350°) until done (about 15–20 minutes). Halve diagonally. Serve hot or at room temperature. Serves 4–6 as a main course. Serves 8–10 Chinese style.

🐖 Fried Pork with Fruit   果 子 肉

$\frac{3}{4}$ lb. lean pork, cut into bite-sized pieces

1 Tbsp. soy sauce

1 Tbsp. dry sherry

2 Tbsps. cornstarch

BATTER

    1 egg, beaten

    2–3 Tbsps. flour

oil for deep frying

3 Tbsps. oil

$\frac{1}{2}$ cup snow peas, stringed

1 cup canned pineapple chunks, drained

1 cup canned loquats, drained

SAUCE

    $\frac{1}{2}$ cup water

    2 Tbsps. liquid from canned pineapple

    $\frac{1}{2}$ tsp. salt

    1 Tbsp. dry sherry

    1 Tbsp. soy sauce

    1 Tbsp. cornstarch mixed with 3 Tbsps. water

Mix pork with soy sauce and sherry, let stand 5 minutes, and coat with cornstarch. Mix BATTER. Heat oil to medium (340°), dip pork in batter, and deep fry until golden brown. Drain. Heat 3 Tbsps. oil, stir-fry snow peas until coated with oil, add pineapple and loquats, and stir-fry 1 minute. Mix SAUCE ingredients in saucepan and bring to boil over medium heat, stirring constantly until thickened. Add fried pork

and fruit and stir 2–3 times. Serve hot. Serves 2–3 as a main course. Serves 5–7 Chinese style.

🍎 Spicy Pork Chops 美味猪肉片

COLOR: PAGE 90

MARINADE
    2 Tbsps. dry sherry
    2 Tbsps. soy sauce
    1 clove garlic, grated
    2 tsps. ginger juice
    2 tsps. cornstarch
4 lean pork chops
3 Tbsps. oil
4 Tbsps. soy sauce
4 tsps. sugar

Mix MARINADE and marinate pork 10 minutes. Heat oil and sauté chops on both sides until done. Add soy sauce and sugar and stir well until liquid disappears. Serve hot. Serves 2 as a main course. Serves 5–6 Chinese style (cut small).

🍎 Fragrant Hills 秋 色

COLOR: PAGE 95

1 lb. lean pork, cut into bite-sized slices
SEASONINGS
    1 Tbsp. dry sherry
    1 Tbsp. soy sauce
    1 tsp. cornstarch
3 Tbsps. oil
1 cup canned or frozen whole kernel corn
½ cup canned whole champignons
1 tsp. salt
½ tsp. sugar

Mix pork with SEASONINGS and let stand 5 minutes. Heat oil and stir-fry pork until color changes. Add corn, champignons, salt, and sugar and stir 3–4 times. Serve hot. Serves 2–3 as a main course. Serves 4–6 Chinese style.

🐷 Sunflower Meat Pies 向日葵餅

COLOR: PAGE 92

FILLING

   $\frac{1}{2}$ lb. lean ground pork

   $\frac{1}{4}$ lb. cabbage, chopped finely and water squeezed out

   1 leek, chopped finely

   1 tsp. ginger juice

   3 Tbsps. soy sauce

   $\frac{1}{2}$ tsp. salt

   1 Tbsp. dry sherry

   2 eggs, beaten and scrambled

3 Tbsps. oil

WRAPPINGS

   3 cups all-purpose flour, sifted

   $1\frac{1}{2}$ cups boiling water

oil for deep frying

Mix all FILLING ingredients except scrambled egg. Heat 3 Tbsps. oil and lightly stir-fry mixture until pork is done (3–4 minutes). Add scrambled egg, mix, and cool. If there is still liquid remaining after cooling, discard liquid.

Add boiling water to flour, mix until smooth, and knead 20–30 times on lightly floured board. Cover with damp cloth and let stand 10 minutes. Roll dough into a long sausage of about 2-inch diameter and cut into 2-inch lengths. Form each slice into a ball and roll out into $\frac{1}{8}$-inch-thick rounds. Place 1 Tbsp. filling mixture in middle of one round, cover with another round, and press firmly to seal edge. Repeat for all ingredients. Scallop edge of each pie as shown in process photos, page 103. Heat oil to hot (360°) and deep fry pies until light brown. Serve hot or at room temperature. Makes 12 pies.

Beef

● Paper-Wrapped Beef　　紙包牛肉

COLOR: PAGE 23

6 oz. beef filet, cut into 24 bite-sized pieces
MARINADE
    1 Tbsp. soy sauce
    1 Tbsp. dry sherry
    dash pepper
24 6-in.-square cellophane sheets (do not use plastic)
2 Tbsps. sesame oil
$\frac{1}{2}$ cup frozen green peas
oil for deep frying

Mix MARINADE and marinate beef 15 minutes. Brush the center of each cellophane sheet with sesame oil, place one slice beef and 1 tsp. green peas on oiled area, fold, and tuck in flaps to secure. Repeat the same process with remaining beef, green peas, and paper. Heat oil to medium (340°) and deep fry wrapped beef until golden brown. Remove from oil and drain. Arrange on serving plate, garnish with lemon slices, and serve hot. Serves 4–6 as a main course. Serves 12 Chinese style.

Note: Paper wrapping should be broken in center, not unwrapped, when ready to eat.

🐄 Chinese Beef Steak 中式牛排

COLOR: PAGE 31

1 lb. beef filet, cut diagonally in 10–12 ¼-in. slices
MARINADE
    4 Tbsps. dry sherry
    2 tsps. ginger juice
    2 tsps. cornstarch
    4 Tbsps. soy sauce
    2 cloves garlic, grated
    dash pepper
    1 tsp. sesame oil
    ½ tsp. baking soda
2 Tbsps. oil
¼ tsp. salt
½ lb. chard or spinach, cut into 3-in. lengths
4 Tbsps. oil
1 tsp. cornstarch, mixed with ¼ cup water
pinch salt
½ tsp. sugar
4 Tbsps. oyster sauce

Mix MARINADE, and marinate beef 15 minutes. Heat 2 Tbsps. oil, add salt, and stir-fry greens 1 minute. Remove to serving plate. Heat oil, and stir-fry beef over high heat until color changes. Combine cornstarch mixture with salt, sugar, and oyster sauce, pour over meat, and stir well until thickened. Arrange on greens on serving plate. Serve hot. Serves 4 as a main course. Serves 6–7 Chinese style.

🐄 Satay Beef 沙爹牛肉

COLOR: PAGE 34

1 lb. flank steak, cut into bite-sized slices (⅛-in. thick)
1 tsp. soy sauce
½ tsp. cornstarch
2 Tbsps. oil
¼ tsp. salt
½ lb. romaine or iceberg lettuce, leaves separated, and torn into 2-in. pieces
2 Tbsps. oil
3 Tbsps. Chinese satay sauce (or 2 tsps. chili sauce)
3 Tbsps. water

Mix beef with soy sauce and cornstarch and let stand 5 minutes. Heat 2 Tbsps. oil, add salt, and stir-fry lettuce over high heat 30 seconds. Remove to serving plate. Heat 2 Tbsps. oil, and stir-fry beef until color changes. Mix satay (or chili) sauce with water, pour over beef, and stir well. Remove from heat, arrange on lettuce, and serve hot. Serves 4 as a main dish. Serves 6–7 Chinese style.

❧ Braised Beef with Eggs 紅燒牛肉

COLOR: PAGE 73

2 lbs. beef shank, cut in 1¼-in. cubes
3 Tbsps. oil
SEASONINGS
 2 Tbsps. dry sherry
 ½ cup soy sauce
 1½ cups water
 1-in. cube ginger, crushed
 3 cloves star anise
4 hard-boiled eggs, shelled
1 Tbsp. brown sugar

Heat oil in deep saucepan and brown beef over high heat. Add SEASONINGS, cover, and bring to boil. Reduce heat to low and simmer 1 hour. Add eggs and brown sugar and continue cooking until beef is tender (about 30 minutes). Remove eggs, halve, and arrange with beef in serving dish. Serve hot with stir-fried vegetables. Serves 4 as a main course. Serves 6-7 Chinese style.

❧ Beef Shashlik 烤牛肉

COLOR: PAGE 84

1 lb. lean beef, cut into 1½-in. cubes
1 stalk leek cut into 2-in. lengths
5 Chinese mushrooms, soaked in lukewarm water until tender, stemmed, and cut into bite-sized pieces
20 water chestnuts
2 Tbsps. soy sauce
2 Tbsps. dry sherry
dash pepper
SESAME SAUCE
 2 Tbsps. sesame paste (or peanut butter)
 2 Tbsps. water
 2 tsps. soy sauce
 1 Tbsps. vinegar
 ½ tsp. salt.
 1 Tbsp. sesame seeds, toasted in a dry frypan over low heat 30 seconds

Thread leek, mushrooms, waterchestnuts, and beef on skewers in that order, until skewer is full but not packed. Sprinkle with soy sauce, sherry, and pepper. Broil under high heat, turning the skewers frequently, for about 10 minutes.
SAUCE: Dilute sesame paste with water until very smooth. Add seasonings and mix well.
Serve hot with sauce. Serves 3 as a main course. Serves 5–6 Chinese style.

Veal with Lotus Root and Peas 小牛肉燉藕

COLOR: PAGE 86

1½ lbs. lotus root, skinned and cut crosswise into
 ½-in. slices
1 Tbsp. vinegar
4 Tbsps. oil
3 slices ginger
1 leek or onion, quartered
1½ lbs. veal, cut into bite-sized cubes
SEASONINGS
 1 Tbsp. dry sherry
 3 Tbsps. soy sauce
 1 tsp. sugar
½ cup green peas

Soak lotus root in water with 1 Tbsp. vinegar 10 minutes; remove and drain. Heat oil and stir-fry ginger and onion 1 minute. Add veal and stir-fry until veal is well coated with oil. Add lotus root and SEASONINGS and enough water to cover. Bring to boil, then simmer over low heat until veal is tender (about 30 minutes). Add green peas 5 minutes before serving. Serve hot. Serves 3 as a main course. Serves 6 Chinese style.

Note: Calf kidneys may be substituted for veal. For 1½ lbs. calf kidneys, use ½ lb. lotus root, sliced very thinly, and 1 cup green peas. Remove fat and "skin" from kidneys and cut into 1-inch pieces. Stir-fry over high heat until done (about 3 minutes), remove to serving dish and discard liquid. Stir-fry lotus root about 2–3 minutes, add peas, stir-fry 1–2 minutes; add to kidneys, mix, and serve immediately.

Beef with Many Moons 月球牛肉

COLOR: PAGE 91

½ lb. lean beef, cut into bite-sized slices
MARINADE
 2 Tbsps. soy sauce
 1 Tbsp. dry sherry
 1 tsp. cornstarch
5 Tbsps. oil
1 cup snow peas, tips broken off, strings removed
4 cups potato chips
1 tsp. dry sherry

Mix beef with MARINADE and let stand 10 minutes. Heat oil, stir-fry beef until color changes, add snow peas and potato chips, stir 2–3 times, and add 1 tsp. sherry. Serve hot. Serves 2 as a main course. Serves 4–5 Chinese style.

🍎 Freckled Hamburgers   珍珠大肉丸

COLOR: PAGE 94

1 lb. ground beef
1 egg, beaten lightly
2 Tbsps. minced onion
1 tsp. ginger juice
1 tsp. salt
1 tsp. sugar
2 tsps. cornstarch
$\frac{1}{2}$ cup glutinous rice, washed and soaked in water 1 hour

Mix all ingredients except rice and form into patties. Sprinkle rice on patties, place on plate, and steam over high heat 30 minutes. Serve hot with mustard, catsup, etc., as desired. Serves 2 as a main course. Serves 4–5 Chinese style (with small patties).

🍎 The Emperor's Favorite Steakburger   天之嬌子

COLOR: PAGE 97

DOUGH
    4 cups all-purpose flour
    2 Tbsps. baking powder
    1 Tbsp. shortening
    $\frac{1}{2}$ cup sugar
    $\frac{1}{2}$ tsp. vinegar
    $\frac{1}{2}$ cup water
MARINADE
    3 Tbsps. soy sauce
    $1\frac{1}{2}$ Tbsps. sesame oil
    1 tsp. cornstarch
7 minute steaks, halved
2 Tbsps. oil
1 head butter lettuce, leaves separated

Mix DOUGH ingredients until smooth and knead on lightly floured board 20–25 times. Form dough into roll 4 inches in diameter and cut roll into 14 slices. Roll out each slice into a flat oval about $6 \times 4 \times \frac{1}{2}$ inches. Line a steamer with damp cheesecloth and steam buns 15 minutes. Mix MARINADE and marinate beef 10 minutes. Heat oil and sauté beef until done. Fold buns in half, insert beef and lettuce, and serve hot. Serves 5–7 as a hearty sandwich. Serves 14 Chinese style.

Soups

● Chicken in Yunnan Pot　汽鍋蒸鷄

COLOR: PAGE 29

1 fryer chicken, backbone removed, and cut into bite-
　sized pieces
5 small dried scallops, soaked overnight
1 cup dried Chinese mushrooms, soaked in lukewarm
　water until tender, stemmed, and cut into bite-
　sized pieces
1 cup canned bamboo shoots, cut into bite-sized pieces
5 cups chicken stock
SEASONINGS
　　4 slices ginger
　　1 stalk leek, cut into 1-in. lengths
　　3 Tbsps. dry sherry
　　1 tsp. salt
　　dash pepper

Place chicken with cold water to cover in large
saucepan and bring to boil over medium heat; reduce
heat to low and continue cooking 1–2 minutes more.
Remove chicken, wash well with water to clean, and
discard boiling water. Place boiled chicken and scallops (with soaking water) in Yunnan pot, add mushrooms, bamboo shoots, stock, and SEASONINGS. Cover,
place pot in steamer, and steam about 3–4 hours.
Serve hot. Serves 2–3 as a main course. Serves 6–8
Chinese style.

Note: Yunnan pot is a lidded earthenware casserole

with pointed chimney rising through the center to the lid to distribute steam evenly (see diagram). A good Duch oven or casserole may be substituted.

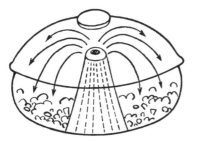

🍎 Melon Soup 冬 瓜 湯

4 cups chicken stock
$\frac{1}{4}$ lb. winter melon, skinned, seeded, and cut into $\frac{1}{2}$-in. cubes
$\frac{1}{4}$ lb. lean pork, diced and sprinkled with $\frac{1}{4}$ tsp. cornstarch and pinch salt
3 medium dried Chinese mushrooms, soaked in luke-warm water until tender, stemmed, and diced
$\frac{1}{4}$ tsp. salt
dash white pepper

Bring stock to boil, add melon, and cook covered over high heat 10 minutes. Add pork and mushroom and cook covered for another 10 minutes or until melon is tender. Season with salt and pepper and serve hot. Serves 4 as a soup course. Serves 5–7 Chinese style.

Note: This cooking time for winter melon is for a melon whose total weight is more than 15 lbs. If a small, tender melon is used, cook melon same amount of time as rest of ingredients—10 minutes. If canned soup stock is used, mix $1\frac{3}{4}$ cups soup stock with $2\frac{1}{4}$ cups water.

🍎 Chicken Wings and Mushroom Soup 鷄 翅 湯

1 lb. chicken wings
4 cups water
12–14 small dried Chinese mushrooms, soaked in lukewarm water until soft and stemmed
$\frac{1}{4}$ tsp. salt
dash white pepper

Place chicken wings in saucepan with water and bring to boil over high heat. Add mushrooms, bring to boil, and reduce heat to medium-low. Cover and cook until chicken wings are tender (about 20 minutes). Season with salt and pepper, and serve hot. Serves 4 as a soup course. Serves 5–6 Chinese style.

137

Thick Vegetable Soup 素菜濃湯

COLOR: PAGE 35

½ cup lighty salted water
½ cup champignons, halved
5 cups water
½ tsp. baking soda
1 lb. chard (or tender potato greens), stemmed
2½ Tbsps. lard (or shortening; but not butter)
4 cups chicken stock
½ tsp. salt
1 Tbsp. oil

Bring water to boil. Add champignons, stir briefly, and drain. Set aside. Bring 5 cups water to boil, add soda and chard leaves, stir, cover, and boil over high heat 6–7 minutes. Remove chard leaves and drain. Rinse well under cold running water. Heat lard, add chard, and mash well over low heat, slowly adding soup stock until mixture is a thick runny liquid (10–15 minutes). Season with salt and remove to serving bowl. Oil on top will keep soup hot. Heat 1 Tbsp. oil, stir-fry champignons 30 seconds, and drop into the center of chard soup. Serve hot. Serves 4 as a soup course. Serves 6–7 Chinese style.

Note: Three beaten eggs may be mixed into chard soup while still on heat. A blender may be used to liquify greens.

Chicken Wine Soup 酒燉雞

COLOR: PAGE 37

1 Tbsp. oil
2 eggs, beaten lightly
3 Tbsps. oil
3 1-in. cubes ginger, crushed
½ fryer chicken, cut into 1½-in. pieces with bone
½ cup Chinese rice wine (or saké)
½ tsp. salt
4 cups chicken stock (or water)
dash white pepper
¼ cup Chinese rice wine (or saké—more or less to taste)

Heat 1 Tbsp. oil in. 6-in. frying pan over medium-high heat, add egg, and fry until set and slightly browned; turn and fry other side until slightly browned. Remove and cut into bite-sized pieces. Heat 3 Tbsps. oil in saucepan, brown ginger, stir-fry chicken over high heat until slightly brown (about 2–3 minutes), add ½ cup wine and salt, and cook 3–4 seconds. Add stock or water, cover, and cook over medium-high heat 15 minutes. Add egg, pepper, and wine to taste, bring to boil and remove from heat. Serve hot. Serves 4 as a soup course. Serves 6–7 Chinese style.

Note: This nutritious dish is traditionally served to women during the first month after childbirth.

❧ Fish Ball Soup 魚丸湯

COLOR: PAGE 36

8–10 fish balls (see recipe, page 50)
6–8 slices ginger
4 cups chicken stock (or water)
6–8 carrot slices
1 small stalk spinach, stemmed and cut in 2-in. lengths
pinch salt
dash white pepper

Place fish balls, ginger slices, and stock in saucepan. Bring to boil over high heat, add carrot slices and spinach, and season with salt and pepper. Bring to boil again, reduce heat to medium, cover, and cook 3 minutes. Serve hot. Serves 4 as a soup course. Serves 5–6 Chinese style.

❧ Clam Soup 蛤蜊湯

10 medium clams
6 cups water
$\frac{1}{2}$ cake beancurd, cut into 18 pieces
1 tsp. ginger juice
1 tsp. salt
1 Tbsp. dry sherry
dash pepper
1 tsp. sesame oil

Place clams that have been washed in several changes of water in a large bowl. Cover well with salted water, add a clean iron nail, and leave at least 3 hours, preferably overnight. This will whiten them and rid them of sand. Wash clams in clean water. Add clams to boiling water. When clams have opened (about 3–4 minutes), add all other ingredients except the sesame oil. Bring to boil again and remove from heat immediately. Before serving, sprinkle with sesame oil. Serve hot. Serves 2 as a soup course. Serves 5 Chinese style.

Note: Clams that do not open have died and should be discarded.

139

❀ Spring Onion and Bean Sprout Soup 豆芽菜湯

COLOR: PAGE 85

¼ lb. lean pork, shred-cut
1 Tbsp. oil
½ cup bean sprouts
5 cups water
1 tsp. salt
1 Tbsp. dry sherry
4 spring onion (or chive) greens, cut into 1½-in. lengths

In a large saucepan, heat oil, and stir-fry pork until color changes. Add bean sprouts, and stir-fry 1 minute. Add water. When liquid boils, remove from heat, and add salt, sherry, and onion greens. Serve hot. Serves 3 as a soup course. Serves 5 Chinese style.

❀ Lettuce and Tomato Soup 紅柿湯

2 Tbsps. oil
½ head lettuce, leaves separated
1 medium tomato, quartered
6 cups chicken stock
2 eggs, beaten

SEASONINGS

1 Tbsp. dry sherry
½ Tbsp. soy sauce
½ tsp. salt

Heat oil in deep saucepan and stir-fry lettuce leaves until tender (about 1 minute). Add tomato, stir 2–3 times, and add stock. Bring to boil, add SEASONINGS, and bring to boil again. Trail beaten egg into boiling liquid, stirring constantly, to form petallike "flakes" of egg. Remove from heat and serve hot. Serves 4 as a soup course. Serves 6–8 Chinese style.

❀ Water Chestnut Soup 荸薺湯

COLOR: PAGE 91

¼ lb. chicken filet, cut into 1-in. slices
1½ cups water
½ tsp. salt
2 cups chicken stock
7 canned water chestnuts, diced finely

Place chicken, water, and salt in saucepan, bring to boil, cover, reduce heat to low, and simmer until tender (about 10 minutes). Add 2 cups stock and water chestnuts and simmer another 3 minutes. Serve hot. Serve in bamboo cups if available. Serves 4 as a soup course. Serves 6–8 Chinese style.

Desserts

🍠 Taro and Gingko Nuts　白果芋头

COLOR: PAGE 38

$\frac{1}{2}$ lb. fresh taro, quartered
1 Tbsp. lard (or shortening; but not butter)
2 cups boiling water
5 Tbsps. sugar (more or less, to taste)
1 Tbsp. oil
$\frac{1}{3}$ cup canned gingko nuts, drained
2 Tbsps. sugar

Steam quartered taro 30 minutes. Remove and cool. Skin and mash well with potato masher. Heat lard over low heat and gradually add taro, mashing until smooth. Increase heat to medium and gradually add boiling water, stirring constantly to make a smooth paste and to keep the taro from sticking to pan. Add sugar and stir until dissolved. Remove to serving bowl. Heat 1 Tbsp. oil and stir-fry gingko nuts over medium heat 2 minutes. Reduce heat to medium-low and add sugar, stirring until melted. Place gingko nuts in center of taro and serve hot. Serves 4 as a dessert course. Serves 5–6 Chinese style.

Note: This confection is traditional and may be a bit starchy for Western taste. Feel free to jazz it up a bit with your favorite fruit brandy or other flavoring.

🌰 Sweet Bird's Nest with Quail Eggs

冰糖燕窩

COLOR: PAGE 38

1 cup prepared bird's nest
3 cups water
1 cup rock sugar or granulated sugar
6 quail eggs, hardboiled and shelled

Put bird's nest, water, and sugar in pot. Bring to a boil, cover, and cook over medium-low heat 40 minutes or until bird's nest is tender, stirring constantly so that bird's nest does not stick to bottom. Add quail eggs and remove from heat. Serve hot or chilled. Serves 4 as a dessert course. Serves 6–7 Chinese style.

Note: Be careful not to overcook bird's nest or it will disintegrate. This recipe is traditional, but the combination of a sweet with eggs may be an acquired taste. The eggs may be omitted and 1½ Tbsps. diced candied ginger and 1 tsp. fruit brandy added for more interest. This dish, drunk as a morning beverage, was thought to give a good complexion and make the skin smooth.

🌰 Sweet Pea Soup

青豆泥

COLOR: PAGE 38

½ cup split or whole dried mung peas (or dried yellow split peas), soaked overnight in ample warm water
2 cups water
⅔ cup sugar (more or less, to taste)
4 Tbsps. cornstarch mixed with ½ cup water

If dried mung peas have skins, remove by rubbing peas between hands in water after soaking. Skins will easily come off, leaving the yellow meats at the bottom of the bowl. Swirl water and carefully pour off water containing skins, taking care not to loose the yellow meat. Place peas in saucepan with ½ cup water, bring to boil, reduce heat to low, and simmer until soft (about 10 minutes). Discard remaining water, if any. Add 2 cups water, bring to boil, reduce heat to medium, and add sugar. Stir until dissolved. Add cornstarch mixture, stirring constantly until thickened. Serve hot. Serves 4 as a dessert course. Serves 5–6 Chinese style.

Note: One-half tsp. almond or lemon extract may be added. If whole mung peas are used, do not soak longer than overnight, since they may begin to sprout.

❀ Coral and Pearls   琥 珀

COLOR: PAGE 89

20 strawberries, washed and patted dry
10 Tbsps. sugar
2 Tbsps. apricot brandy

Combine sugar and brandy, and melt over low heat, stirring constantly. Dip strawberries in glaze then immediately in cold water to harden. Drain.

10 canned water chestnuts
2 Tbsps. sugar
5 Tbsps. sugar
1 Tbsp. apricot brandy
powdered sugar

Cover water chestnuts with 2 Tbsps. sugar and let stand overnight. Combine 5 Tbsps. sugar and brandy and melt over low heat, stirring constantly. Dip water chestnuts in the glaze then immediately in cold water to harden. Drain. Arrange glazed strawberries and water chestnuts together on serving plate and sprinkle with powdered sugar. Serves 4–5 as a dessert course. Serves 10 Chinese style.

❀ Autumn Treasure   秋 紅 玉

COLOR: PAGE 89

6 medium tart apples, peeled, cored, quartered lengthwise, and cut into $\frac{1}{3}$-in. slices
4 Tbsps. Mao-tai-chiu or Lao-chiu liquor
3 Tbsps. sugar
5 slices lemon peel
STREUSEL TOPPING
    $\frac{3}{4}$ cup lard
    $\frac{1}{2}$ cup sugar
    1 cup flour
    1 egg yolk

Place apple slices in buttered baking dish and sprinkle wine and sugar over apples. Dot with slices of lemon peel. Bake in medium oven (350°) 10 minutes. Do not overbake. While baking apple, mix lard with sugar until crumbly. Add flour and egg yolk and with fingers mix well into crumbs. Arrange the streusel mixture over apple and bake another 15–20 minutes, until golden brown. Serve hot. Serves 6 as a dessert course. Serves 10–12 Chinese style.

Note: Sherry or brandy may be substituted for Chinese liquors.

❀ Walnut Cream 核桃酪

2 cups whole walnuts, shelled and blanched
oil for deep frying
3 cups water
1 cup rock sugar
½ cup cornmeal
3 cups water

Heat oil to medium (340°) and deep fry walnuts very briefly. Take care to remove walnuts as soon as color changes to avoid scorching. Drain on kitchen paper and pat dry. Place walnuts with 3 cups water in blender. Blend until about the consistency of fine cornmeal. Line colander with cheesecloth, pour walnut liquid through cheesecloth, reserving liquid. Squeeze walnut pulp in cheesecloth to obtain all liquid and discard dry pulp. Add walnut liquid to sugar and cornmeal, and boil 10 minutes, stirring constantly. Gradually add 3 cups water, stirring constantly to form a smooth heavy liquid, like eggnog or a cream soup. Serve hot. Serves 4 as a dessert course. Serves 6 Chinese style.

❀ Date Pudding 蒸蛋糕

COLOR: PAGE 98

1 cup dried Chinese dates, soaked in water 2–3 hours and drained
2 cups crumbled pound cake, sponge cake, or raisin bread
4 cups milk
¾ cup sugar
1 Tbsp. butter
¼ tsp. salt
3 eggs, lightly beaten
SAUCE
    2 Tbsps. sugar
    1 Tbsp. cornstarch
    1½ cups water
    ½ Tbsp. fruit brandy or ½ tsp. vanilla (optional)

Place dates in bottom of lightly buttered bowl. Soak cake in milk 30 minutes. Mix all ingredients except SAUCE, pour over dates, and steam until firm (about 20 minutes). Cool and invert bowl over serving plate. Mix SAUCE ingredients in saucepan over low heat and stir until thickened. Pour over pudding and serve. Serves 4–5 as a dessert. Serves 10 Chinese style.

🍎 Smiling Boys

開口笑

COLOR: PAGE 98

BATTER

    2 cups all-purpose flour
    ½ cup sugar
    2 tsps. baking powder
    1½ Tbsps. shortening
    2 eggs, beaten, ¼ set aside
    ½ cup water
½ cup black sesame seeds
½ cup white sesame seeds
oil for deep frying

Blend BATTER ingredients well (including ¾ of beaten egg). Form into 1-inch balls, dip balls in ¼ of beaten egg, and roll ½ of balls in black sesame seeds and ½ in white sesame seads. Heat oil to medium (340°) and deep fry until surface of balls split. Makes about 24–28 balls.

🍎 Egg Crepes Almond

杏仁鷄蛋卷

COLOR: PAGE 98

3 eggs, beaten
2 Tbsps. sugar
8 Tbsps. all-purpose flour
½ cup milk

pinch salt
2 Tbsps. finely chopped blanched almonds
2 Tbsps. sugar
1 apple

Combine egg, sugar, flour, milk, and salt and blend well. Heat a lightly oiled 6- or 9-inch frying pan over medium heat and make 4–5 crepes of medium thickness, frying both sides until just light brown. Set aside. Heat frying pan over medium heat, add almonds, stir-fry 10 seconds, add sugar, and stir 10 seconds more. Spread 1 Tbsp. almond-sugar mixture in center of each crepe, roll, and cut into ½-inch slices. Cut apple into notches as indicated in the color photo, arrange into bee or butterfly design, using crystal sugar or bits of angelica or cherry for the eyes. Serves 3–4 as a dessert. Serves 6–8 Chinese style.

145

🍑 Sesame Torte　　芝蔴糕

COLOR: PAGE 98

4 egg whites, beaten until glossy and stiff
4 Tbsps. white sesame seeds, toasted lightly and rough-
　ly ground in mortar
4 Tbsps. sugar
pinch salt
2 Tbsps. all-purpose flour
½ tsp. vanilla or almond extract (optional)
whipped cream

Sprinkle all ingredients except whipped cream over beaten egg whites and gently fold in. Turn out into lightly buttered 8- or 9-in. cake loaf pan and bake in 375° preheated oven until firm but still moist (about 15 minutes). Cool. Cut in half to form two layers (or repeat process with same amount of ingredients to bake another layer). Frost generously with whipped cream. Cut as desired. Serve 4 as a dessert. Serves 8 Chinese style.

Note: The thin strips of torte in the color photo were cut that way just to make a nice design. Actually the cake should be completely frosted with whipped cream. This recipe makes a rather thin layer.

Glossaried Index

Taro (山芋; Japanese: *tororo*). Somewhat different from the Polynesion taro tuber (see photo, p. 43). Becomes sticky when grated. Available fresh in Oriental groceries.

sweet, and gingko nuts, 141

tea, Swatownese. This is included mainly for interest and because a Swatownese tea setting is pictured in the color plate of page 32.

Tea is to the Swatownese as whiskey is to the Irish and wine to the French. Swatownese tea cups are very small and are placed on a pewter box with a perforated lid, through which liquid can drain. Boiling water is used to rinse a small teapot. Tea leaves ($1\frac{1}{4}$ tsp. per person) are steeped about 2-3 minutes. Just before pouring the tea, the cups are rinsed with boiling water and the water drained into the pewter box.

Tea is poured rapidly from cup to cup without halting the flow. Two circuits of the tea cups should empty the pot. If the flow is halted, air will enter the teapot and let the aroma escape.

tomato

and lettuce soup, 140

stuffed, 58

torte, sesame, 145

turnip(s)

dried, preserved, 55

tidbit, 55

Veal, with lotus root and peas, 134

vegetables, mixed

abalone with, 76

braised, 60, 62

chicken and, 115

salad, 57

stir-fried, 63

vegetable soup, thick, 138

vermicelli, transparent (粉糸). The Chinese form of these transparent filaments is different from the the Japanese (*harusame*), but the latter may substitute. Should be soaked before using. Do not overcook. Also, do not confuse with Italian vermicelli.

and carrots, 65

with eggs, 107

Walnut(s), 49

cream, 144

prawns with, 73

water chestnuts (荸薺; Japanese: *kuwai*). Available canned. Of course use this favorite crisp vegetable in any dish you want.

deep fried, 49, 52

glazed, 143

soup, 140

winter melon (冬瓜; Japanese: *tōgan*). A firm-fleshed, hard-skinned green melon that develops a frosty film on the skin. Rather bland in flavor, but combines well with other vegetables. Also pickles and crystallizes very well.

soup, 137